REAPPROACHING PAUL

REAPPROACHING PAUL

by Morton Scott Enslin

THE WESTMINSTER PRESS
Philadelphia

Book Design by
Dorothy Alden Smith

Published by The Westminster Press ®

Philadelphia, Pennsylvania

PRINTED IN THE UNITED STATES OF AMERICA

Library of Congress Cataloging in Publication Data

Enslin, Morton Scott, 1897-
    Reapproaching Paul.

            Includes bibliographical references.
            1. Paul, Saint, apostle.   I. Title.
BS2506.E57   225.9'24 [B]   72-4941

                        ISBN 0-664-20951-3

TO RUTH
cor unum, via una

CONTENTS

FOREWORD

I have made no attempt in this little volume to cite older and contemporary scholars for support, for refutation, or even for the purpose of indicating that I was not unaware of them, for in a work of this sort it would seem pedantic. Scholars who may be inclined to read these pages, if only to refute some of my unorthodox assumptions and conclusions, will be familiar with the omitted literature; the general reader, and the reader who either knows nothing about Paul or else dislikes him, will neither need nor want it. Notes have been kept to a minimum. Greek has been almost entirely omitted from the text and is rare even in the notes. When a word does occur, it should be no obstacle to those who cannot use it. It is hoped that readers, both professional and lay, will be charitable enough to realize that this omission of specific references to the plenitude of books and articles remotely and even immediately related to matters considered in the present volume is no proof positive that I have not read them or even profited from them. In my attempt to stress matters that seem to me important and to emphasize matters that I think significant for a fresh approach to Paul, I have sought to avoid cluttering the text with materials not essential for my purpose. Nor am I inclined to append either a bibliography or indexes. The former, if at all comprehensive, would be disproportionately long and for the most part—at least for many readers—of little value; the latter appears to me quite unnecessary, for in no sense is this volume either a commentary intended to illumine the occasional Biblical citations or so complicated as to warrant sampling in the place of connected reading. Whether these decisions are wise or unwise must be determined by the reader himself.

M.S.E.

1 | INTRODUCING PAUL

Setting our sights

A half century ago it was the fashion to write books entitled "Jesus and Paul" or "Jesus or Paul." In consequence, the popular pictures of the two central heroes, both unique in Christian history and affection, stood clear: Jesus was the founder, establisher, of the resultant Christian church, for which he had lived and died; Paul was in a real sense its second founder and its greatest theologian. In the eyes of some there was regret that this latter fact was the case, for to them Paul, influential though he had become, was really a liability. It was he, they were sure, who had muddied the clear waters; and in consequence there was a current, or at least an undercurrent, of desire which may be styled "Back to Jesus" and which virtually meant "Away from Paul."

Today there is a bit more restraint toward both of these emphases. Jesus lived and died a Jew, with his eye fixed on the speedy coming of the new age promised to Abraham and long awaited by Abraham's children. Paul, too, was a Jew and remained such throughout his stormy life. He had been converted, but not from Judaism to Christianity—for there was no such thing in his day—but to what he was convinced was the true Judaism, an unqualified obedience to and deathless love for God's greatest gift to man, Jesus Christ, the complete and final revelation of himself and his will for men.

It has become a commonplace that to write a biography of
Jesus is impossible. It has become increasingly clear, however,
that Jesus had exerted so deathless a grip upon many about
him that their confidence that he had been sent by God to do
as he had done could not be destroyed by the cross on which
he had died. Instead, their confidence led them to continue his
work, assured that he would speedily return to consummate
what he had begun. And in this confidence the nature of their
crucified prophet and master came to be seen in a new per-
spective. In a word, the Jesus of history became the Christ of
faith. In no small degree this has proved the perfect tribute.
Not his death and its unexpected reversal, but the life he had
lived by the lake in Galilee and on the streets of Jerusalem
made it inevitable that the first disciples and the many generations which have followed them found it natural to see in him
the embodiment and reality of their God-blessed dreams and
hopes. As many have come to see, at times painfully, it is not
possible to identify the Jesus of history with the Christ of
faith, as earlier generations sought to do. Each succeeding
generation has painted him in its own colors, always confident
that the resulting portrait gave reality and certainty to their
own longings and dreams. Not that, but something far better
resulted: the historical Jesus made the Christ of faith not only
possible but inevitable. That is a triumph and treasure beyond
price.

Paul has not fared so well. To many, he was singularly and
conspicuously blind to the values that they have come to prize
in the stories about and the words of Jesus. Instead, he substituted a medley of "things hard to be understood" (II Peter
3:16), seeking to prove them by words of Scripture which he
wrenched violently from their context and which would seem
again and again to oppose, not support, his positive assertions.
At times he was boastfully condescending; always he was passionate and ready to heap abusive names on all who were res-
tive under his heavy hand and arrogant self-confidence. This
latter could lead him to insist that anyone—be he man or

angel—who preached a gospel variant from his was worthy of
and certain to receive damnation. A thoroughgoing opportunist and utterly lacking in anything approaching real humility,
he stands far removed from the one he claimed to serve but
failed to understand. In addition, to many a Jew who has
come to appreciate, if not to revere, Jesus, Paul stands as the
age-old Esau, minimizing his birthright and rejecting his heritage. Paul's words seem to them shocking and incredible in a
son of Abraham and only to be explained as coming from one
physically and spiritually remote from Zion.

Some of these strictures, while far from being mine, I can
understand, for, as an undergraduate in a theological seminary,
I had come to know—and thoroughly dislike—Paul as an arrogant and muddleheaded theologian. To discover him in what
was (to me) a new role was a moving experience, and it remains as vivid today as it was, now fifty years ago, during my
years of graduate study with James Hardy Ropes at Harvard,
when I first began to see that in this case, as so often, prejudice was largely due to ignorance. Through the years this discovery has been increasingly manifest, with Paul one of my
dearest friends.

Many elements in Paul's teaching are no longer in our world
and outlook. He seemingly divided the life of Christ into three
sections: from the first beginning, in heaven; a descent to
earth to dwell for a short time in a human body and to suffer
death on a cross; a resurrection in a spiritual body, with an ascent to heaven, whence he appeared to several, including
Paul, and will speedily return. For us, most of this is impossible—at least it is for me. Despite our gospel songs, we do not
expect a return on the clouds. The notion of a spiritual body is
to us meaningless, if not downright crude and unthinkable.
Copernicus doomed, for thinking men, notions of an ascent to
heaven and a return therefrom on the clouds. *Kenōsis,* as Paul
seems to phrase or utilize it in Phil., ch. 2, is at best artificial;
and without it preexistence, which in itself is meaningless in
any real sense, would turn Jesus into a living lie. Elements like

these—I have listed but a few—are surely dispensable without loss. But Paul is not to be modernized any more than we are to be archaized. Paul lived, and very effectively, in the first century, not the twentieth. Many of the problems which concerned him have long since lapsed; many more which trouble us today were definitely not in his horizon, and it is idle to try to see them there.

Today interest in Paul seems once more ascendant. But while many of the studies are of real interest, it appears to me that there is still too great emphasis on an aspect ·of Paul which, if prominent, is still not essential. Too long he has been seen as primarily a theologian, and one conspicuous tendency in the currently revived concern is to make him a thoroughly logical thinker. His letters, and at times even their sections, are being rearranged to indicate a steady growth and development. Paul was not primarily a theologian but a man with an unusual ability to weld groups together into lasting wholes. To overlook or minimize this concern and his amazing ability to realize it is to fail to see the real Paul and to lose sight of much that is still of great value in his·legacy to us.

The debt Christianity owes to Paul is threefold, and each part is concerned with human conduct. Over against the Jew, Paul insisted upon freedom from the Law. Too often we have viewed this insistence upon freedom as reckless abandonment of values and an opened gate to antinomianism. Rather, it was aimed at the attempt of men trying to justify themselves by their keeping of the Law and thereby gaining as their right what God alone in his grace could bestow. This insistence was not hostility to the content of the Law, which Paul deeply prized and ever employed, but to the way in which men mistakenly sought to use it in support of their arrogant claims, instead of realizing that all they had and were came from God as his most gracious gift. A second fundamental emphasis was Paul's unending, always central, protest against the laxity of morals in the Hellenistic world where he felt bound to labor. Christianity's deepest debt to Judaism was, and still is, to be found in its insistence upon the sturdy Jewish morality with its stress upon the purity of family life. Nor were these two demands alone. In addition, Paul struck the note of the fellowship (*koinōnia*) of believers, not alone with the Lord, but with their fellow believers. The vertical tie demanded the horizontal. Here Paul was a pioneer. The Greek speculative systems, where many of the values Paul stressed were also to be found, were woefully weak here, with little or no attempt to organize their followers into local groups or to stimulate them to life. Jesus, the wandering prophet, had seemingly not stressed this demand either. He had had no thought of founding a church or establishing churches. His aim had been the challenge to readiness for the kingdom speedily to dawn.

Paul formed organic entities bound by the closest of ties to a living source whose members would materially stimulate one another to the utmost. His plan worked. And that basic emphasis is as sound today as it was nineteen centuries ago. To neglect this central emphasis, because the sections wherein it is conspicuous are often at the end of his letters, is to lose sight of the real Paul. As did his Master, he might think the world was going to end on the morrow—and time has shown they were both wrong in that belief—but in sober truth Paul taught as if it was going to last forever. And when an inexperienced group of new converts in Thessalonica accepted his theological heralding of the speedy dawn of the kingdom and not unnaturally ceased work to live on their friends—"You can't take it with you!"—Paul's word was not uncertain: they were to study to be quiet, to quit gadding about, to work with their own hands. A later disciple, writing in the master's name and modeling his word upon that of his teacher, hit the same note even more clearly:

> If any will not work, neither let him eat. For we hear of some that walk among you disorderly, that work not at all, but are busybodies. Now them that are such we command and exhort in the Lord Jesus Christ, that with quietness they work, and eat their own bread. (II Thess. 3:10-12.)

In some of his theological bursts Paul may be sounding notes which no longer speak to our condition, but words such as these are as needed and pointed today as when Paul first gave them utterance—despite the fact that (perhaps better, because) our politicians seem so completely to have forgotten them. It is this Paul, so often neglected by the theologians into whose possessive hands he has fallen, that I have sought in the following pages to reapproach through his letters.

2 | GATEWAY TO PAUL

Our sources for approach

Both Jesus and Paul died by violence, martyrs to the cause
for which they had devoted their lives. And, as has so often
been the case, their deaths added luster to their lives and
aided them to gain an ever-increasing immortality of memory
and influence. *De mortuis nil nisi bonum* has often proved no
idle word but again and again has swayed the verdict. It has
often happened that "of the dead nothing but good" is spoken. Socrates in Athens, Jesus in Jerusalem, Paul probably in
Rome, Abraham Lincoln in Washington, Martin Luther King
in Memphis, Robert Kennedy in Los Angeles—in each case
one might say that the person whose hand gave the hemlock,
drove the nails, or pulled the trigger, while scarcely a conscious friend to his victim, nonetheless aided the victim to rise
above a growing dissatisfaction and in many cases a lessening
influence, to achieve a fame in memory's eye which proves fast
against fading.

As the years passed, both Jesus and Paul came to be figures
to achieve attention on the written and printed page, but this
was far from true in the early years. As for Jesus, first in the
letters of Paul, later in the Gospels and other Christian writings—he came to occupy a central place; but one looks in vain
for even the bare mention of his name in the writings flowing
from the pens of historians and litterateurs of his own day.

Whereas Jesus was quite unmentioned by Josephus in any of his writings about events in the land of Palestine at the time of his ministry and death, a later Christian sought to remedy that inconceivable omission by an inserted paragraph of labored concern.[1] When at the end of the century the Roman historian Suetonius records a disturbance in Rome which led Claudius to take measures against the Roman Jews, he mentions a Chrestus as the chief troublemaker, evidencing his total ignorance both of the incident itself and of its cause.[2]

Nor is the matter different for Paul. Eventually a Christian writer sought to chronicle Paul's work in spreading the gospel in the world of the Gentiles, but no mention of him is to be found in the writings of this larger world. Again, a later writer in the fourth century sought to remedy this amazing omission with a labored correspondence between Paul and Seneca, in which he sought not only to make the Roman appreciative of Paul but to bring him into the Christian fold.

When it comes to sources of knowledge, we are thus definitely limited. So far as Jesus is concerned, our sole supply of material is the late record of fragments orally reported of what he had said and what he had done. Jesus himself had written nothing, nor is there any indication that any of his immediate followers attempted any written record. This is not surprising. Sharing his confidence that the end of the age was at hand, to dawn at any moment, his followers had little concern to pass on a record to subsequent generations, for there would be no subsequent generations. In addition, his earliest disciples were all Jews, with an inherited confidence that in the Scriptures was contained God's complete and entire revelation. Torah was not restricted to a body of laws, as non-Jewish generations have so mistakenly believed, misled by the rendering of *torah* by *nomos* in the Greek translations of the Old Testament and subsequently by *law* in the resultant English versions. Torah does not, and did not, mean legislation or law; rather, it was an almost all-embracing term signifying the whole of God's revelation, thus containing all that God had made known of his nature, character, and purpose. All that ever was to happen was therein to be found. It might be written, so to speak, in invisible ink. It was there nonetheless, and it was Israel's privilege and duty to make explicit what was there implicit. Thus the oral law, styled in Mark's Gospel "the tradition of men," was not anything new or alien being read back into God's pronouncements; rather, it was the God-directed and all-important bringing to light of what he had purposed, planned, and recorded in this all-embracive revelation which he had given men—more properly the Jews—as his gift beyond compare.

Thus, of course, there never was a time when the followers of Jesus were not convinced that in this all-inclusive revelation, not only as to what men should do but of all that ever was to be, were clear indications both of their teacher and of the movement he had started. Failure to recognize this fundamental confidence has led to easy ridicule of "messianic interpretation," which saw Jesus and his doings, the cross and the Gentile mission, all written in the pages of old and begging for recognition. Was not Joshua ("Jesus," when we read in Greek) Moses' great successor who led Israel across the Jordan into the Promised Land? Was that not proof positive that Jesus was the greater Moses? When God had said, "Let us make man in our own image," to whom was he speaking? Of course he was speaking to Jesus, as the prologue to the Gospel of John so confidently stresses. God never changes, is never confronted with new and unforeseen happenings. What is happening now is but the outcome of what he had purposed and planned. More than that, not only had he planned it but he had revealed it for those who had eyes to see.

With that background of belief, the early followers of Jesus had full confidence that their history was therein to be found. Christianity started as a movement in Judaism and never forgot that fact, even as the ways between synagogue and church became farther and farther apart. Jesus' followers were the true Judaism, faithful to the promises and demands of God. The

Bible, full of predictions of them and their movement, was actually *their* book, not the possession of blind and hostile Jewry, for, as Justin Martyr insisted to his Jewish opponent, Trypho, "We believe it as you do not." [3]

Thus for decades after Calvary there was apparently no thought of writing any sort of "Christian" history or any sort of Life of Jesus, for all that was of moment had been written already by God himself. Apparently in the months and years which followed Calvary, that which was central for Jesus' followers was the constant challenge to sound the proclamation of their crucified leader, so that when he returned, as speedily he would, he would find faith in the earth. At first there was the confidence that this interval would be very brief, and its brevity drove them to their task: "So much to do, so little time." As the years passed, the conviction grew that God had not failed to keep his promise, still less that Jesus had been mistaken in his proclamation. Rather, the delay was to enable all men to hear and believe. As Paul was later to phrase it, "A hardening in part hath befallen Israel, until the fulness of the Gentiles be come in; and so all Israel shall be saved" (Rom. 11:25-26). When this had happened, then would come the end.

From the start, Christianity has been a missionary religion, going along highways and byways and seeking to compel men to come in; fifty years ago the leaders might phrase themselves, "The world for Christ in this generation," but this was no new note: it has been the theme from the earliest days. In those days of early missionary activity, apparently many of the preachers had buttressed their words and illustrated their message by words and stories of Jesus as they had learned them from the growing tradition. In the form of short, crisp "And he said's" and "And he did's," these gave both color and authority to their preaching.

In the course of this usage the tradition varied and grew. There was no written record to be quoted without alteration. The tradition was not in the form of scriptures to be revered; it was, rather, in the form of windows to let light in. Thus, of course, the material grew and changed. "And he said" came to be cast in forms indicating when and why he so said; "and he did" similarly became modified and expanded. Names came to be introduced. The unnamed individual, "one of the by-standers," who had drawn his sword and had cut off the ear of the servant of the high priest, became specifically "one of those with Jesus" and finally "Simon Peter." The luckless serv-ant became "Malchus"; the ear became the "right" ear, and it was miraculously healed by Jesus. The two thieves crucified with Jesus, who both railed at him, came to be differentiated into good and bad, giving rise to later lush additional modifi-cations. It is not surprising that when we have the same para-ble reported in more than one Gospel—notably the "talents" and the "pounds"—variations and modifications are to be seen.

Nor are the variations and developments restricted to stories, whether parables or accounts of things done. They are equally evident in the recorded teachings. Many readers have been shocked at the thought of this and have sought to explain the variations by assuming a repetition in variant form by Jesus himself. Thoughtful reading of the words now standing in the mouth of Jesus in the four Gospels should convince any-one who reads with his mind as well as his eyes that they have undergone change and modification. That the same man could have phrased himself (as reported in the first three Gospels) in crisp parables and crystal-clear pronouncements about the coming kingdom of God, with a minimum of reference to him-self, but also (as in John) in long, turgid declamations on the theme "I am . . . ," is utterly beyond belief. Fifty years ago saw a welter of writing by forerunners of our modern psychia-trists. These doctors, several of them superintendents of insane asylums, with no training in history—literary or otherwise— sought to take all four Gospels as unaltered firsthand clinical reports. In consequence, they concluded that any individual who could give utterance to these utterly contradictory words must have been mentally unbalanced, oscillating between *grand* and *petit mal*. Fortunately that epidemic of unconse-crated ignorance was brought to an end, not by the outraged protests of pious Christians but by literary ("higher") critics who convicted the would-be medical historians of having grossly misused writings which they were definitely unqualified to attempt to handle. That they had misused the Gospels was evident in their treating them as clinical on-the-spot reports by medically expert nurses and physicians and thus ready-to-hand for exact medical diagnosis.

Thus the Gospels, while a rich heritage—lovely strings of priceless pearls—are far from being sources from which we can write a biography of Jesus. We do not know when or where he was born, how old he was at his death, nor how long he had acted as God's prophet of the coming end. Whenever we have stories about him—notably the lovely birth stories, the visit of the twelve-year-old boy to the Temple at Jerusalem, the threefold temptation at the hands of Satan—we recognize that to take them as sober factual prose is to deprive them of their priceless worth. We may be able to get a possible picture of the sort of man he was, the general nature of his work and message, the impress he was able to make upon those who heard and reverenced him; but to attempt a biography from materials such as these, the products of decades of repetition and change, is fruitless. Very possibly in the materials we have, amid many changed and added bits, are words preserved with little change; but it is quite impossible to be sure which these are. To some that has been a sad loss. To them it may be said: The stories, the words, the insights still remain in the Gospel pages, undimmed and undenied. Truth is truth, quite regardless of who says it. That the words are of value only if uttered by Jesus is a conclusion as unwarranted as is its fellow, "It is true because God said it." Our experience has surely brought us to the far sounder and more rewarding insight: "God has been seen to have said it because men have come to believe it to be true and of value."

Paul did not escape this recasting which was the lot of Jesus. The one picture that was painted of him and that has left its definite impress on most of the "lives" subsequently written is in the book of Acts. We refer to the second part of the combined writing, Luke-Acts, which traces the rise and spread of what we now style Christianity from its start in Galilee to its establishment in the great centers of the Mediterranean world. In several sections of the part devoted to Paul, who is set forth as the one chiefly responsible for the success of the movement among Gentiles, a curious change occurs. Without warning, the form of the narrative changes from the descriptive third-person "they" to the seemingly personal first-person "we." It was not unnatural to argue that the author was himself one of the Pauline company and thus the recorder of what he had himself seen. One point—and to me an all-important one—is often overlooked or at least minimized. This gifted and facile writer who has given us our sole connected account of Paul and his doings is the one who was most free in his recasting Jesus. It is unnecessary to stress this indisputable and well-recognized fact. Thoughtful reading of the first three Gospels—Mark, Matthew, and Luke, commonly styled the Synoptic Gospels—should be sufficient to convince any open-minded reader that "Luke" has unhesitatingly rewritten his "sources" in view of what he conceived to be the real first step to the Gentile mission. This was no new or sudden step on the part of disciples who found Jerusalem too hot to remain in after their leader's death. Rather, it was part and parcel of God's unfolding plan, to be discovered at every step of the way, had man only eyes to see. It had been foreshadowed by the chorus of the angels to the shepherds at the time of the Savior's birth:

> Glory to God in the highest and on earth,
> Peace to the men of his choice.
> (Luke 2:14.)

It had been blessed and furthered by Jesus himself, first in his opening words at Nazareth, then in his endorsement of Samar-

itans. It had been glimpsed in the scene at Pentecost with its
assembled multitude, in the word of Peter to Cornelius, of
Paul before the Areopagus, in Paul's final word at Rome. From
the opening page of the Gospel to the closing page of Acts
(what a pity that the continuity of this book should have been
broken by the insertion of the Gospel of John between its two
sections!) there is thus a steady and orderly advance. It is all
a part of the eternal purpose of God, who knows the end from
the beginning, and of whom it cannot be said, "He repented
himself and made a new beginning." In the first part of this
story (i.e., the Gospel) we can see the way he utilized and
unhesitatingly recast his sources and added to them. The high
probability is that he showed no greater restraint in the second half of his writing (i.e., Acts).

It is commonly felt that the sources for this second half have
vanished and can, at best, be tentatively inferred from the resultant text, in view of the way Luke treated Mark and Matthew—or, as many would prefer, Mark and Q. I have long
been convinced that another source, and a principal one, for
Luke was the letters of Paul, which he both knew and utilized without acknowledgment.

Unlike Jesus, who left no writings and thus can be seen only
through what others wrote about him, Paul did leave letters,
although one would never know this all-important fact from
the chronicle in Acts. And these letters are our one firsthand
and reliable source of information of his words and doings.
More and more this has been in part recognized. Riddle and
Knox insisted, now many years ago, that to see Paul one must
look to his letters, not to the account in Acts. Many other
scholars, agreeing in part or in whole with this contention,
have sought to make the letters their quarry, but again and
again they have essentially qualified this proper demand.
They have conceded that, since here and there Paul's own
words confirm this or that statement in Acts, there is likelihood that other of "Luke's" statements, while not expressly
confirmed by the letters of Paul, are probably correct.

To my mind, these modest qualifications are ill-advised and of a sort to minimize, or at least lessen, the basically proper demand: "If you would know Paul, study his letters." The conspicuous silence in Acts regarding the letters of the one whom Luke chose as his principal hero has long troubled scholars. Whether Luke did or did not know the letters of Paul may seem to many to be open to question. To me, as I have argued at some length,[4] it is incredible that Luke did not know and highly improbable that he did not use them. Long before Luke-Acts was published, the scattered letters of Paul had been collected and were in use. Paul's letters had set the fashion for Christian writing, and the so-called General Epistles, not to mention the seven letters to churches strangely present in our canonical Revelation, would certainly seem to be reflections of them. That they were early regarded as written to seven churches—Rome, Corinth, Galatia, Ephesus, Philippi, Colossae, and Thessalonica—is not to be forgotten in noting that the resultant General Epistles and the intrusive correspondence in Rev., chs. 2 and 3, are also seven in number. The often-sounded note that after his death Paul went, forgotten, into a limbo of neglect, only to be rescued by the Lukan pen, is most unlikely. Rather, I should be inclined to see in the story in Acts the utilized reflection of Paul's prominence and letters, not the cause of a later fame.

Thus the only question is: Why did Luke remain silent about Paul's letters, although frequently mentioning letters written by others, as James to the church in Antioch or Claudius Lysias to Felix? The only answer at all likely is that he deliberately refrained from mention of them—although perfectly ready to draw from them as his principal source—because, first, the letters were already being turned to an improper use by unorthodox opponents, and, second, while they provided Luke with material which he could easily recast, they were not of the sort to make direct quotation advisable. Instead of dramatic incidents and crisp parables there were blistering reproofs, constant correction, and long-winded theological arguments. None of this was of a sort to appeal to our creative writer. Still worse, they might well clash with the picture he was drawing of the essential harmony among Christians. Thus from every angle—Paul's constant correction of his churches and of the tragic clash with Jerusalem; the fact that Paul was now in the embrace of heretics who were misusing his letters—quotation from, or even mention of, the letters was unwise. Instead, Luke utilized them and made them serve his fundamental purpose.

To the seemingly obvious objection, so often made, "If Luke had known the letters, he would surely have made greater use of them," the answer is easy. In addition to the reasons suggested in the preceding paragraph, there is amazingly little in the letters that would have lent itself to detached repetition, not to mention exact quotation. But the charge of "little use" appears quite unwarranted. In my judgment Luke used them very fully. Back of almost every incident he paints is a statement or basis for inference in one or more of the letters quite sufficient for a writer who was an author, not a copyist or restricted editor.

The famous list of sufferings and hardships which the exasperated Paul cited in II Cor., ch. 11, has been put to very effective use by the author of Acts in his catena of trials and hardships encountered by his hero. That an author is ignorant of everything he does not mention—an objection so often raised even today by writers indignant that their own articles and books are unnoted by the author they are at the moment attempting to review—is an argument which has only to be phrased to be seen as absurd. After all, authors can omit what they do not want or what they find themselves unable to utilize for lack of space—a possibility particularly of moment in the days before leafed codices, when the length of a usable scroll was of no small concern. This same type of argument is frequently raised by champions of the independence of Matthew and Luke. It is easy to forget that during the first century, when much of the material now in our New Testament was being written, none of it was regarded as "canonical," and thus secure against modification or alteration. Two thousand years of increasing veneration has put much of it in the position to seem, even to the most thoroughgoing critics, of a sort not-to-be-omitted-if-known. Luke could not have omitted or broken up the Sermon on the Mount, had he known it. Matthew could not have refrained from using the parables of the prodigal and the good Samaritan, had he known them. Luke could not have failed to tell the story of Onesimus or the contest of Paul with the wild beasts at Ephesus, had he known them. This type of argument, despite its frequence, is not impressive. What it really means is, "We could not so do." A little more realistic attention to the difference made through the lapse of two millennia might well lessen the feeling of need for the invention of imagined, but long-vanished sources, be they L, M, Q, or their many fellows. We shall have occasion to consider these matters in greater detail later. For the moment, the foregoing must suffice to indicate my contention that, far from being unknown or unused, the letters of Paul (and not Luke's memoirs as a fellow traveler) appear to have been the principal source used by Luke in reconstructing the activities of the man who brought to reality the Gentile mission. Luke employed Paul's letters in full accord with a type or tone of writing, long familiar to every Biblical critic: what *should* have been; what *must* have been; what *was*.

Another warning is not out of place. There is danger involved in using the Lukan mélange as the frame into which insights from the Pauline letters are to be placed and, too often, slanted. This section of Acts contains several speeches in the mouth of Paul. Too often these speeches are regarded as, and even styled, "Paul's own," and then treated as essentially firsthand material. No classical student will need to be warned against this peril—but too often, readers of the Bible, professional and lay, are not "classical students." Such students will well remember the crystal-clear word of Thucydides:

As to the speeches that were made by different men, either when they were about to begin the war or when they were actually engaged therein, it has been difficult to recall with strict accuracy the words actually spoken, both for me as regards that which I myself heard, and for those who from various other sources have brought me reports. Therefore the speeches are given in the language in which, as it seemed to me, the several speakers would express, on the subjects under consideration, the sentiments most befitting the occasion, though at the same time I have adhered as closely as possible to the general sense of what was actually said.[5]

It were well for the reader of Acts (and of the Gospels!) to remember this honest confession, which practice was not peculiar to Thucydides but could have been described with equal honesty by Josephus, Philo, Livy, Tacitus, and their many colleagues. He will not be perplexed by the so-evident similarities between all the speeches of Acts, be they by a Peter, a Stephen, or a Paul. He will not be inclined to debate whether Paul has been "petronized" or Peter "paulinized," for he will realize that all of them have been "lukanized." Their sameness of tone, their smoothness and freedom from those little idiosyncrasies that style the man himself, the amazing ability of the author to know what was said in a secret council (ch. 4:15-17), the providential preservation of the letter of the centurion, Claudius Lysias, to Felix, with its sympathetic and highly satisfactory statement of Paul's influence (ch. 23:26-30) —all this requires no labored explanation. The speeches without exception are the author's convenient means for providing the reader necessary information. Occasionally they may give us a fair picture of early Christian thought and the sort of preaching that early Christians heard; they are not firsthand sources of knowledge for reconstructing a life of Peter or of Paul. None of the speeches attributed to Paul reveals the Paul known to us from his own letters. Even in the farewell speech of Paul to the Ephesian elders at Miletus (ch. 20:18-35)—a speech regarded by some critics as different from the others

and perhaps actually a part of the perplexing "We" source—
there appears the stereotyped prophecy of impending evil:

> I know that after my departing grievous wolves shall enter in
> among you, not sparing the flock; and from your own selves
> shall men arise, speaking perverse things, to draw away the
> disciples after them. (Acts 20:29-30.)

The tenor of this passage is so exactly similar to that of the
Pastoral Epistles, Jude, II Peter, Matt. 5:10-12 and 10:16-23,
that it does not seem rash to consider this too a prophecy very
definitely *post eventum*.

So far as their "historical accuracy" is concerned, again the
probability is that Luke's handling of the speeches of Paul is
of a piece with his whole literary construction and that he
would have failed to understand the modern distinction between what should be and what was. Three speeches in the
earlier pages of Acts are not without value as indications of his
free use of material and imagination.

1. In Peter's first speech he is made to describe (not to later
readers but to his fellow Jews in Jerusalem) an incident that
had purportedly just happened and that they must have
known of as well as he did, in the following amazing language:

> And it *became known* to all *the dwellers at Jerusalem;* inso-
> much that *in their language* that field *was called* Akeldama,
> that is, The field of blood. (Acts 1:19.)

2. In James's speech at the council of Jerusalem, James is
made to quote Amos 9:11-12 in a very free paraphrase of the
Septuagint. The Hebrew reads:

> In that day I will raise up the tabernacle of David that is
> fallen, and close up the breaches thereof; and I will raise up its

ruins, and I will build it again as in the days of old; that they
may possess the remnant of Edom, and *all the nations that are
called by my name,* saith Yahweh that doeth this.

That is, that Israel may possess Edom and the other nations.
But James (Acts 15:16-18) is made to say:

That the residue of men may seek after the Lord,
And *all the Gentiles,* upon whom *my name is called* . . .

That James of Jerusalem used the Septuagint is most unlikely;
surely Gal. 2:11 ff. makes it highly improbable that this utterance represents James's attitude, to say nothing of his words.

3. In his oft-quoted advice, Gamaliel (Acts 5:35-39) is
made to refer to the rebellion of Theudas which had occurred
"before these days" and which, he goes on to say, was later
followed by the insurrection and death of Judas of Galilee.
Now Theudas raised his rebellion in the days of Festus and
thus not earlier than A.D. 44—that is, several years later than
the difficulty which prompted Gamaliel to utter his warning.
Furthermore, Judas of Galilee raised his rebellion not *after*
Theudas, but nearly forty years *before* (A.D. 6). That this
speech was never uttered by Gamaliel but was composed by
Luke to indicate what, in his judgment, Gamaliel *ought* to
have said, and therefore *did* say, is too obvious to require
argument.

Thus the high probability is that in Luke's use of speeches
purportedly by Paul, the same readiness of composition and
occasional slips of historical accuracy are to be seen. In short:
we are unwilling to distort the Paul of the letters by forcing
him onto the Procrustean bed of Lukan narrative; neither
should we allow the speeches of Paul composed by Luke to
obscure the letters composed by Paul. The speeches may, of
course, occasionally have historic value, but are wisely not to
be used as source material for moot points—still less as slant-

ing or correcting Paul's own written statements. In a word, we are not safe in using them unless they agree exactly with something else, the authority for which is unquestioned. In that case they are superfluous.

3 | DAMASCUS: AFTER AND BEFORE

Paul, what manner of Jew?

When we turn to his letters, our one real source for information about Paul and his doings, there are many natural questions left unanswered. Nonetheless some very important
points can be marked on our graph, and from them a reasonably accurate curve may be plotted. Of his early years little is
known: when and where he was born he never intimates, and
to seek to fill in this lacuna is simply to guess. That he was a
Jew of orthodox parents and circumcised on the eighth day;
that he was proud of membership by birth in the tribe of Benjamin; that he, and presumably his parents, followed the
teaching of the Pharisees in the interpretation of Torah, as did
most Jews; that he was strict to the point of fanaticism in his
reverence for the Jewish law and traditions; that he joined
heartily in persecuting the early followers of the crucified
Jesus at Damascus: this is the sum of our knowledge of his
pre-Christian days.

Then in Damascus his sky fell in. He became convinced that
he was wrong, was opposing God, in this devoted opposition;
that God was blessing the movement and that in his opposition, although sure that he was doing God's service, he had
been in awful fact opposing those under God's blessing, and
thus had been opposing God himself. From persecutor he
swung to the exact opposite, becoming an ardent champion of

the one he had sought to destroy. Following a three-year period—undescribed, but very conceivably of work—in Arabia
and Damascus, he had made a short trip to Jerusalem to visit
Cephas (Peter). Then he spent several years in what he styles
"Syria and Cilicia." Next we find him in Antioch, where he
seemingly had come to be prominent among, if not the leader
of, Christians there. During these years (how long they were
is less certain, as we shall see, than is commonly supposed) he
had become convinced that in the movement he was now so
zealously championing there was a place for Gentiles and that
God in his overall direction had intended them as Paul's particular field of service. He had gone to Jerusalem and despite
some opposition had been recognized as a missioner in that
field. During the next few years—perhaps also in those preceding, which he briefly mentioned as being spent in "Syria
and Cilicia"—he had traveled widely in Asia Minor and eastern Europe (Macedonia and Greece), establishing churches.
Paul had kept in contact with those churches he had organized and for whom he clearly felt both responsibility and
affection, by means of letters written to answer questions and
if possible correct difficulties. While he never describes this
travel in any detail, those of his letters which have come down
to us allow a fair "plotting of the curve," making clear that he
had visited Galatia, Asia, Macedonia, and Achaia. Mention is
made in those letters of specific cities—for the most part cities
of real prominence and strategically located, such as Philippi,
Thessalonica, Athens, Corinth, Ephesus, Colossae, and Laodicea. These references, together with occasional chance words,
enable us to get a pretty clear general picture of the world in
which Paul and his lieutenants worked. Finally he became
convinced that he should seek further fields to the west. He
dreamed of going as far as Spain, with an interim stop in
Rome—not to establish a church in Rome, for such was already in being, but to greet its members en route to his new
field of endeavor. But before this departure for the West he
desired to make another trip to Jerusalem, not improbably in

the hope that such a visit and the gift he was bringing them from the Gentile churches that he had established would further allay opposition and suspicion of both him and his churches, which might otherwise well show itself when he was no longer in the area.

Here our direct information ceases. Romans would seem to be the last letter from his pen. It has often been assumed that Philippians, Colossians, and Philemon were written from Rome. There is no hint in any direct word of Paul's that this is the case; nor is there anything in any of these letters themselves demanding or even suggesting a Roman residence. The Pastoral Epistles are recognized as definitely both post-Pauline and un-Pauline, and thus have no light to cast on the matter. The curtain falls on Paul as he pens this last letter from Corinth, a letter apparently intended for all the churches for which he had labored. Indeed, he seems to have directed that a copy be sent to Rome to acquaint them with his plans and to disabuse them of wrong impressions they had apparently received both as to his orthodoxy and his reason for coming to them. Tradition (that is, the concluding section of Acts) adds the familiar story of his trip overland to Jerusalem, of the miscarriage of his hopes, of his arrest and two-year imprisonment at the provincial capital, Caesarea, of his dramatic appeal to Caesar as a Roman citizen, of the sea voyage to Rome as a prisoner, and of his two-year stay under house arrest in the nation's capital. But of all this there is no hint in Paul's own words. I have argued that for Luke, as for us, Paul's letters are his chief, if not his only source; that there is nothing in Luke's account of Paul which cannot be inferred, either reliably or by interpretive expansion and alteration, from Paul's own writings. If my contention is correct, then the nature and source of these concluding chapters, for which there is no clue from Paul, must remain uncertain. That both Peter and Paul eventually reached and perhaps died in Rome has long been the confident belief. In the absence of any direct evidence to the contrary, this is quite possible. It must nonetheless be asserted that because this Lukan coda, especially the vivid tale of the voyage and shipwreck, "sounds natural" is no indication of anything more than the unquestioned competence of Luke as a gifted author who can style himself and plead his case with a high degree of verisimilitude.

This picture of Paul's career, which is transparent in his letters when they are examined both critically and appreciatively, can, as will subsequently be indicated, be filled in with considerable detail from other words and allusions in the letters. And it has the virtue of being solid and factual. It may well be that many of the additional elements and stories in the Lukan picture are so attractive and endeared through the centuries of their repetition that when so rigorously excluded we miss them and feel the resultant picture is, as it confessedly is, incomplete. It is easy to style their exclusion as irresponsible denial of solid external tradition. It is precisely at this point that I vigorously demur. That they consist of solid and "external tradition" appears to me unproven and unprovable. Rather, they would appear to me what may be better styled "internal inference." When the author wrote, many years after Paul had passed from the scene, he had the Pauline letters and he sought from them to pen a connected picture of the man chiefly responsible for what appeared to him the one truly great story, the rise and development of the Gentile mission. From the materials before him he read in and read out and produced his deathless saga. That it is superb writing none may soberly deny; but that it is free from Luke's basic insistence—"what should have been, must have been, was"— that, I submit, is simply an unknown and unproven hypothesis. To omit his lively stories may be costly; to use them as the guidelines within which Paul and his letters are to be forced is to risk losing Paul, and that is folly.

Luke's craftsmanship enabled him to articulate usable material from the epistles into an essentially continuous account of Paul's career, where one step leads logically and continuously to the next. This continuity is a striking characteristic of the whole of Luke-Acts, and is clearly indicated by the author in his famous preface (Luke 1:1-4). No better example of this is to be found than in what may be styled "Paul's pre-Damascus days." In Paul's letters (Gal. 1:17) our first glimpse of him is at Damascus. No hint is given as to why he chanced to be in that city nor from where he had come. These lacunae Luke skillfully fills in, in all probability, as it seems to me, not from independent knowledge or "available tradition" but by deduction and inference from the letters themselves. Thus, Paul was a citizen of Tarsus, had in fact been born there; thence he had gone to Jerusalem, where he had been a pupil of Gamaliel. He had been present at the stoning of Stephen, had later gone from Jerusalem, armed with letters of authority from the high priest there to Damascus. As he had neared the city, his dramatic conversion had taken place.

Occasional critics have been hesitant to accept some of these details—notably the time of study with Gamaliel, for little or nothing in his letters suggests the sort of training likely at the hands of the learned teacher.[6] Certainly the way Paul is introduced into the confused account of Stephen's death is at best stilted and awkward. Nevertheless, the birth and presumable upbringing in Tarsus are details that have been widely and uniformly accepted even by critics most insistent that it is from Paul's letters alone that we can safely derive our picture. So John Knox can write:

> The same thing can be said about the second item—Paul's birth in Tarsus. This, too, rests only upon the testimony of Acts (22:3). But again there is no obvious reason why Paul should have mentioned it and no plausible reason why Luke should have invented it (as a matter of fact, he would probably have preferred that Paul come from Jerusalem); and there is no competing suggestion. That Paul was born in Tarsus is in line with the general impression the letters give that their author was an extra-Palestinian Jew, as well as with his specific statement in Gal. 1:21 that Cilicia was one of the early

fields of his evangelistic work. Although then, we can be fully sure only that Paul was a Hellenistic Jew, for this is all the letters tell us, we can be reasonably certain also that he was Saul of Tarsus in Cilicia.[7]

To me this seems far from certain and appears to be a very dangerous and unwise denial of Knox's central and proper insistence. As will be indicated presently, there seems to me a very plausible reason why Luke should have invented it, namely, the very revealing word of Paul to which Knox himself refers. But before considering the matter of Luke's possible source of knowledge, an even more important point needs attention. It is not an overstatement to say that probably no other single detail has been more important in shaping popular appraisals of Paul than this word of his birth in Tarsus. This, and not "the general impression the letters give," has led to the confident styling of Paul as a Jew of the Diaspora who, through contacts, perhaps education, in a "Hellenistic university town" had been alienated from the traditions of his fathers. For this reason he could speak slightingly of the Jewish law and discard it as "refuse"—as no unspoiled Jew brought up under the shadow of Zion could do.

In recent years there has been a lot of speculation—and often pontifical pronouncement—about "Hellenistic Judaism" and its differences from what has been styled "normative Judaism." With this easy assumption of a birth and upbringing in Tarsus it has been increasingly common to put Paul in that setting and to read out of his letters seeming confirmation of what we have unconsciously first read in. Actually it is just as plausible to reverse the argument. Precisely because he was brought up in a land well outside the direct influence of Zion, there could well have been an even greater zeal shown by his pious parents. Aware of the dangers at every turn, they would strive to make fragrantly vital a heritage beyond compare and to safeguard it against the allures of the fleshpots of Egypt— their zeal even greater than might have been normal to those hedged about with the security of Zion.

In the perplexing story in Acts of the difficulties that arose in Jerusalem in consequence of the appointment and activity of the seven men among whom Stephen was prominent, there is one note that is often overlooked. The opposition which Stephen encountered was apparently not from native Jerusalemite Jews—not, to use the convenient phrase, representative of "normative Judaism"—but from those who were members of the "synagogue[s] called [the synagogue?] of the Libertines, and of the Cyrenians, and of the Alexandrians, and of them of Cilicia and Asia" (Acts 6:9). When one is indulging in the framing of hypotheses—and glittering generalities about the nature and outlook of "diaspora Jews" in general and Saul of Tarsus in particular are most certainly of that sort—he should realize the possibility that those in Jerusalem who took offense at the activity of Stephen and his fellows were apparently "diaspora Jews" who had settled in Zion for the precise purpose of getting free from the contaminating danger of the larger world. In a word, if we are free to frame hypotheses, we are free to theorize that these synagogues of "Hellenistic Jews" were ultraorthodox, composed of those who had at last been able to return to Zion, and that their reason for disputing with Stephen was due to a feeling of outrage that some of their own members had become infected with a sorry heritage. Certainly it would not be the first, or last, occasion when a local synagogue or church that had been placidly unconcerned about such matters as heresy and the ill effects upon simple piety incident to a college education suddenly awoke to the fact that one of their own younger members had contracted that same sorry disease. What had been a matter of little concern suddenly took on real meaning.

I am not arguing that this is the case of these groups in Jerusalem, for I am far from sure that Luke's picture of them, of their actions, and of the whole incident involving Stephen, is in any sense an untouched photograph. I am, however, insisting that in lieu of any definite evidence to the contrary, it is as plausible a hypothesis regarding the outlook and actions of some Hellenistic ("diaspora") Jews as is the one so easily noised about today that all Jews of the Diaspora must have been far less Jewish than their fellows in Judea. Easy generalities are, and always have been, dangerous, as was evidenced a few years ago by the charge by Ben-Gurion that of necessity all Jews today who are content to live outside Israel must be atheists.

Thus, to me, easy characterizing of Paul as a poor Jew, to whom the proud inheritance into which he had entered had lost value, due to his upbringing in the Diaspora, is without warrant and utterly mischievous. I do not question that Paul wrote these words in Philippians:

> . . . though I myself might have confidence even in the flesh; if any other man thinketh to have confidence in the flesh, I yet more: circumcised the eighth day, of the stock of Israel, of the tribe of Benjamin, a Hebrew of Hebrews; as touching the law, a Pharisee; as touching zeal, persecuting the church; as touching the righteousness which is in the law, found blameless. Howbeit, what things were gain to me, these have I counted loss for Christ. Yea verily, and I count all things to be loss for the excellency of the knowledge of Christ Jesus my Lord: for whom I suffered the loss of all things, and do count them but refuse . . . (Phil. 3:4-8.)

Nor am I surprised that these words have been regarded as outrageous and unforgivable blasphemy by many a Jew who is now increasingly disposed to a more favorable judgment of Jesus. When this passage is taken out of context, not only the context of this particular letter, but of Paul's whole thinking, this apparent minimizing of values beyond price and styling them not only "loss" but "refuse," together with what seems an almost contemptuous dismissal of the law, God's greatest gift, and of circumcision, the proud badge of God's covenant—all this makes talk easy about Paul being at best a very poor Jew, spoiled by his contacts in the Diaspora, where, like the earlier Esau, he had despised his birthright.

But neither the words in Philippians, nor the picture of Judaism read out of Galatians (itself a passionate and exaggerated letter in which Paul is using, at times abusing, every argument possible to win his contention, and which he was later to regret and definitely recast and correct), nor occasional other phrases that we have now in black and white throw any light whatever on how Paul felt before his shattering experience in Damascus. The reason why he subsequently came to a position in which he could so express himself we may for the moment reserve. But we should do it with eyes wide open to the fact that these words were penned years afterward: they throw absolutely no light on his days before he changed to champion the one he had so zealously sought to destroy.

To deny—much more, to prove the denial—that Paul was born or had at least lived in Tarsus[8] would be both pointless and absurd. It can be asserted that there is nothing in Paul's letters to suggest it and that there is no evidence, apart from Luke, to support it. The question then arises: Where did Luke obtain this bit of geographical information connecting Paul with Tarsus? Did he get it from "sources" known to him which subsequently vanished without a trace or did Paul's own words provide the clue to the fertile imagination of the versatile Luke? To me the latter possibility is the more likely.

In his rapid review of the events following his conversion in Damascus Paul remarks that after a short visit to Jerusalem to see Cephas he went "into the regions of Syria and Cilicia" (Gal. 1:21). That those years were devoted to zealous preaching of the cause he was now championing is certainly implied by the following verses, but no details of this story are known. The striking fact is that Luke, too, passes in silence over this lengthy period in what Paul had laconically styled "Syria and Cilicia":

And when the brethren [sc. in Jerusalem] knew it, they brought him down to Caesarea, and sent him forth to Tarsus. (Acts 9:30.)

And he [sc. Barnabas] went forth to Tarsus to seek for Saul; and when he had found him, he brought him unto Antioch. (Acts 11:25-26.)

Is it not more than curious that Luke passes in silence over this one period in Paul's ministry—a long period, too—for which he could get no further information from the letters? He summarizes it with a word:

So the church throughout all Judaea and Galilee and Samaria had peace, being edified; and walking in the fear of the Lord and in the comfort of the Holy Spirit, was multiplied. (Acts 9:31.)

This word sounds surprisingly like a simple paraphrase of Paul's similar word in Galatians:

And I was still unknown by face unto the churches of Judaea which were in Christ: but they only heard say, He that once persecuted us now preacheth the faith of which he once made havoc; and they glorified God in me. (Gal. 1:22-24.)

Thus I am inclined to see in this clear evidence that Luke is here, as elsewhere, definitely dependent upon Paul's letters for his information. He passes.in silence over this long period, not because he knew some tradition which was curiously laconic or because for some obscure reason he himself was content so to compress it, but because his one source of knowledge, Paul's letter, provided no detail. Nor is it to be overlooked that for Paul's "Syria and Cilicia" he substituted "Tarsus." Tarsus was the chief city of Cilicia. Is it not highly likely that we can read Luke's thoughts at this point very exactly? Had not Paul gone back to his home town prior to his real period of work?

In the early pages of the Gospel, Luke had unhesitatingly rewritten the gospel story by recasting the story of the rejection in Nazareth (Luke 4:16-30), which both Mark and Matthew had set later in the ministry (Mark 6:1-6; Matt.

13:53-58). For Luke it is the all-important prelude to the ministry and sounds the note to be so constantly heard as the narrative proceeds—the Gentile mission. Thus without hesitation Luke recasts the Markan outline—perhaps following a hint from Matthew (Matt. 4:13)—by making this visit of Jesus to his home town prior to his ministry by the Galilean lake. That this rearrangement is highly effective in his narrative is too obvious to require argument; that it indicates his entire readiness to rearrange and change his sources is not to be denied.

Similarities in what may be styled scholarly techniques are not to be lightly disregarded. Instead, it appears to me highly probable that Luke understood from Paul's laconic mention of "Syria and Cilicia" that he, as Jesus before him, had returned to his home. And since Tarsus was the chief city of Cilicia, he both substitutes it for Paul's "Syria and Cilicia" in this borrowed passage, and finds it natural to have Barnabas go subsequently to Tarsus to bring Paul to Antioch (Acts 11:25), and in a later speech has Paul refer to himself as "a Jew, born in Tarsus of Cilicia" (Acts 22:3). If this reasoning is sound, it would not seem hypercritical to conclude that, were it not for Luke's fertile imagination and ability to discover answers to his questions by making seemingly explicit what was at best implicit in his sources, these details would never have been known to us. As one ponders the history of Biblical criticism, both ancient and modern, he is likely to feel that Luke is far from unique in this respect.

In this connection two other points may be stressed. As already noted, Luke represents Barnabas as the one who many years later brought Paul to Antioch. Seemingly he felt that the entire period had been spent there by Paul, which in itself raises many baffling problems if the incidents so rapidly referred to in Gal. 1:10-22 are to be regarded as a chronological series. For the moment we can defer considering many of these patent difficulties. The point of immediate concern is the linking of Paul and Barnabas in them. In the second trip to Jerusalem, Barnabas accompanies Paul (Gal. 2:1). In the incident immediately following, the dispute with Cephas in Antioch, Barnabas is there too and falls under Paul's displeasure (Gal. 2:13). This trip to Jerusalem has regularly been understood as from Antioch, although recently Riddle and Knox have challenged this view. Certainly Luke so records it. But quite independent of Luke, the following incident, as Paul refers to it, beginning with the words, "But when Cephas came to Antioch" (Gal. 2:11), would certainly seem to suggest an incident which took place following the trip, and most naturally in the same place from which the earlier trip had started. Disregarding for the moment other problems regarding Antioch, and the probability that a part of the years in "Syria and Cilicia" may have been spent there, it appears to me that it is this repeated reference to Barnabas in Antioch which led to the somewhat improbable Lukan story that Barnabas had been the one sent to fetch Paul from Tarsus. To Luke there was the real problem of accounting for Paul's return from Tarsus and presence in Antioch, where Gal. 2:11 places him. Again I am inclined to feel that Luke found his material for his reconstruction in Paul's words. Paul is brought to Antioch —not Damascus or Jerusalem—for in this next incident in his Pauline sources that is where Paul is found. And the reason he had left Tarsus is neatly explained. The references to Barnabas and to Paul's evident fondness or respect for him—"even Barnabas was carried away with their dissimulation" (Gal. 2:13)—make the story of Barnabas being sent to fetch Paul a natural connective.

Between Paul's birth in Tarsus and his conversion near Damascus, as Luke records his career, stands a chapter in Jerusalem, quite unmentioned or hinted at in Paul's letters. I have suggested that this whole "pre-Damascus" picture in Acts is not improbably to be seen as due to Luke's creative genius, not to his own memories or sources, now lost, which he utilized, and I have examined in some detail the problems involved in his mention of Tarsus. It is now necessary to consider the other two items—the days at the feet of Gamaliel and the connection with Stephen. The latter, far more important in the eyes of Luke, may well be looked at first. To appreciate its importance in the structure that Luke is rearing, a bit of repetition is necessary.

At the start of the narrative that we style Luke-Acts stands the story of the rejection at Nazareth (Luke 4:16-30). In this carefully and artfully constructed passage is expressed the theme or motif that is to occur again and again throughout the two-volume work. In a very real sense it may be styled the melodic note; it may also be called very definitely apologetic. Throughout the first part—our Gospel—Luke is at pains to prove that Jesus was the true Jewish Messiah. He had come to the Jews, had been born of the seed of David; but they had rejected him. Christianity was the new Israel. Gentile Christianity had arisen not through wanton neglect on the part of Jesus to go to the Jews. Far from it; he had gone to them, but they had rejected him. This is the framework for the whole of the Lukan writing and accounts for its prominent position at the start of the Gospel. From the materials in Mark 6:1-6 and a quotation from Isaiah, Luke reconstructs this incident to sound the note, "Salvation has come to men," placing a speech on this theme in Jesus' mouth. This theme had been present in the world from the moment of the Messiah's birth and had been hymned by the heavenly host (Luke 2:14); now it was openly and clearly fulfilled. Although those to whom Jesus preached—even his immediate followers—failed to realize it, this salvation was for all men irrespective of race or status, Jew or Gentile, strict adherent of the law or outcast. Thus, Jesus is made to refer to two prophets' experiences with Gentiles—Elijah with the widow of Sarepta, and Elisha with Naaman the Syrian.

Thus Luke strikes the chord which is to sound again and again throughout the whole story of the rise and development of Christianity and which is more fully orchestrated in the de-

veloping score. At the time of Stephen's death the real break
comes: the actual start of the Gentile mission is clearly made,
as the deliberately repeated word (Acts 8:4; 11:19) so clearly
shows. But, as Luke takes pains to point out, this is no new or
unhinted change or development. At Pentecost there had been
a clear foretaste of it; furthermore in Jesus' own ministry the
start had been made. Jesus had clearly revealed his attitude,
not alone in sending out the seventy, a patent parallel to the
twelve, and in the choice of Samaritans—the only Gentiles
with whom he could come in contact—but in his first address.
The lengthy and artificial section, Luke 9:51 to 18:14, the so-
called "journey section," so often earlier clumsily styled the
"Perean Ministry," would seem intended by Luke as a parallel
to the Galilean ministry. It is deliberately placed by Luke as a
sequel to the Galilean ministry at what is not only the logical
place but the one place where it will least disrupt the Markan
structure, thus sounding the melodic note that Jesus' ministry
was for all men, as the aged Simeon had predicted:

> A light for revelation to the Gentiles,
> And the glory of thy people Israel.
>   (Luke 2:32.)

Thus at the very opening Luke strikes the note and continues
it to the last page of the work, where Paul, after quoting the
apposite word of Isaiah, is made to conclude:

> Be it known therefore unto you, that this salvation of God is
> sent unto the Gentiles: they will also hear. (Acts 28:28.)

Though the mission started from Jerusalem, the channel
through which it reached the uttermost parts of the earth was
Paul. This Luke expands in the second half of the account. In
order to join these two strains and to make the latter the out-
growth of the former, he brings Paul into connection with
what he has chosen as the start of the Gentile mission, namely,
the martyrdom of Stephen.

The abrupt appearance of Paul in the story of the death of Stephen, and the inconsequential part he plays in it, certainly arouse the suspicion that the author has worked over a story which originally had no mention of Paul in order to connect Paul with the event which he is making the start of the movement of which Paul became the chief agent. It also provides background for Paul's own word as to his activity as a persecutor.

Having definitely connected Paul with Jerusalem and the persecution there—surely the mention of Paul's previous study with Gamaliel, for which there is no trace in any of Paul's own words, serves simply as the explanation of why the Tarsan Jew was in Jerusalem at the time of Stephen's death—Luke tries to reconcile this redrawn picture with the historical fact, seemingly clear in Paul's word to the Galatians, that Damascus, not Jerusalem, was the place where the abrupt right-about-face took place. The young Saul, after laying waste the church in Jerusalem, turns for further worlds to conquer, and, armed with letters from the high priest, he sets out for Damascus. Again, were this episode to be regarded as historic fact, problems would arise. The precise value of these letters, which in any case would hardly have come from the high priest himself, but from the Sanhedrin of which he was the presiding head, would be obscure. They could hardly have been more than letters of introduction, since the Sanhedrin's actual authority did not extend beyond the border of the Roman province of Judea. It would be difficult to imagine the Roman authorities in Damascus recognizing their validity or consenting to any very active persecution by the Jerusalem emissary.[9] But with these details Luke is not concerned. His effort is to provide a plausible explanation of Paul's hostility and to reconcile it with the tradition of his Damascene activity—both of which were attested by Paul himself.

At this point another query arises. To what extent did Paul's days in Damascus prior to his years in Syria and Cilicia influence later tradition? It appears to me not unlikely that, had it not been for Paul's own memory, here expressed in Galatians, neither we nor Luke would have known anything about them. Once again it must be repeated: To see Luke here following "sources" which were known to him but which subsequently vanished without a trace is surely more cumbrous than the admission that Paul's own words had provided the guides for the story and that Luke's own fertile imagination, never hampered by restrictive historical facts or dates, contrived the consequent tale.

Nor is this arbitrary union of two different strains without precedent in Luke's writing. We have already seen an apparent example of it in his recasting and interpretation of Paul's unexplained trip to Syria and Cilicia as a return home, prior to the start of his real mission, as a parallel to Jesus' own return and rejection at Nazareth, the latter so manifestly a creation by Luke himself. An even sharper parallel may be seen in the two so similar unions Jerusalem-Damascus and Nazareth-Bethlehem.

In Luke, ch. 2, we have the lovely story of Jesus' birth in Bethlehem. With this tradition, also given by Matthew, Luke is familiar, and as he writes his account he accepts it. But while Matthew gives no intimation that Jesus' parents had lived elsewhere and, instead, expressly states that after their return from Egypt they emigrated to Nazareth to escape the attention of Archelaus (Matt. 2:22-23), Luke is aware of the tradition that Nazareth, not Bethlehem, was the original home of Joseph and Mary. Yet Jesus, great David's greater son, had been born in Bethlehem. To bridge this difficulty, or rather to connect two divergent and contradictory traditions, he introduces the census of Quirinius, which did not take place until after the deposition of Archelaus, to explain how it was that folks had left their home in Nazareth at so critical a moment. To this end he rewrites the story, recasting the matter of the census—both its scope and date—and introducing the detail of the birth in a manger or cattle stall, which is, of course, not found in Matthew's account, where the birth takes place in a house, presumably the home of Joseph and Mary. My critics could easily charge that it is poor criticism to introduce one debatable point to prove another. This possible objection is hardly apt. To close one's eyes to obvious parallels of literary construction, and to try to cast an ancient author (one who is striving to pen a continuous and growing account) in the role of a modern historian (whose one endeavor is—or should be —not to slant facts to accord with his own notions): this is scarcely a rewarding approach to a work like Luke-Acts.

Together with the reference to Tarsus as the birthplace of Paul is the repeated reference to him as "Saul." Again this detail is limited to Acts, for Paul never alludes to it; but it too has been widely accepted, even by the most critical. Twenty times in Acts, Paul is styled "Saul"; of these, fifteen are in the Graecized form Saulos; five in the transliterated Saoul, this latter only a vocative in the mouth of the resurrected Jesus or of Ananias, who according to Luke had aided in Paul's recovery after the conversion trauma (Acts 9:10-19). Save for three of these vocatives—all in later speeches by Paul referring to his conversion—this is the only way Paul is referred to until the story of the conversion of the proconsul of Cyprus, Sergius Paulus, following the denunciation and blasting of Elymas (Bar Jesus) the magician, in the first incident detailed by Luke of his hero. And in this, the last of the fifteen, come the words, "But Saul, who is also Paul" (Acts 13:9). From then on throughout the narrative, whether of his exploits in Gentile territory or in Jerusalem, he is always referred to as Paul. This matter, considered superficially, is of but trivial concern. The one thing that makes it of possible significance is the seeming import Luke gives to it in what is scarcely a casual or accidental treatment.

Twice Paul refers with pride to his ancestry in the tribe of Benjamin.[10] The first Israelite king, Saul, son of Kish, was the most prominent member of this tribe. Thus, to most students, the fact that Paul bore this Jewish name has not seemed un-

likely (quite apart from such questions as to whether the actual descent—were books of genealogies according to tribes
available at this date?—is factual or due to proud family
tradition). That Jews often had Gentile names as well as Jewish, and that these often resembled each other, e.g., Jason-
Joshua (Jesus), is too well known to need argument.

The one matter of concern in this superficial and petty problem is Luke's source of knowledge. Did he find this minor detail in other sources then available to him or did he deduce it,
as we so easily can, from these two words in Paul's letters? If
we accept, as most apparently do, the first of the two hypotheses, the question then arises: If Paul from his earliest days
had both names, when and what led him to prefer the Latin-
ized Paul? That the change was Paul's own and due to mod-
esty (the Latin adjective *paulus* means "little"), as Augustine
surmised,[11] or that it was in connection with his Roman citi-
zenship—another item never mentioned or claimed by Paul
but known to us solely from Luke—these are but profitless
guesses.

As Luke tells the story, his interpretation is clear. The man's
name was Saul; the change to Paul was another right-about-
face.[12] It came when this man started his Gentile mission.
Whether the first convert, as Luke tells the story, was actually
Sergius *Paulus* (Acts 13:7) or whether this is a literary detail
invented for the purpose is debatable. But the fact that he was
always Saul until this incident, and always Paul thereafter, is
certainly to be seen as a deliberate literary touch. Naturally,
when Paul is made to refer back to his conversion experience
and to quote the word of the Lord to him, the latter speaking
Hebrew had hailed him by the name he then bore. Thus I am
forced to conclude that here, as so constantly, it is quite unnecessary to search afar for long-vanished sources available to
Luke. This point which he deduced and of which he made so
effective use lies crystal-clear although unexpressed in Paul's
own writing. Nor is it without interest that in the one other
place where a Saul is mentioned in Acts—Paul's speech at

Pisidian Antioch—Luke's phrasing of the reference, "And God gave unto them Saul the son of Kish, a man of the tribe of Benjamin" (Acts 13:21), suggests that he is consciously emphasizing that the Saul who is speaking was also a Benjaminite, and that he has deliberately used the Hebrew spelling of the name (Saoul) to avoid confusion with the other one-time Saul.

To me the evidence seems plain. The common denial—a quite recent insistence[13]—that Luke knew or used the Pauline letters needs fresh consideration instead of automatic repetition. As I have tried to show, there is no detail in the story Luke tells of Paul's days prior to his conversion which he could not have deduced from the material in the letters. To those enamoured of the quest for vanished sources and to whom the more complicated and obscure and less likely is always preferable to the simpler and more obvious, all this will likely seem most unacceptable, especially since it would view Luke as an author with ideas, not a slavish compiler who can repeat but never revise or invent. Both in theology and the examination of writings long since canonical, the more obscure and too often the more unlikely has a fatal charm. For such, Tertullian's oft-quoted *Credo quia absurdum* still has point.

4 | PAUL'S ABOUT-FACE

"Last of all he appeared to me also"

> For ye have heard of my manner of life in time past in the
> Jew's religion, how that beyond measure I persecuted the
> church of God, and made havoc of it: and I advanced in the
> Jews' religion beyond many of my own age among my coun-
> trymen, being more exceedingly zealous for the traditions of
> my fathers. (Gal. 1:13-14.)

With these words, a prelude to his change of heart due to
what he was sure was a revelation of God, Paul makes his first
appearance to us. To see these as the words of a "diaspora"
Jew who really was not a Jew at all but had been alienated
from the tradition of his fathers through contacts in a "Hellenistic university town" requires a degree of (un)historical
imagination which is quite beyond me. Nor is there, as I read
his epistles, a hint of any pre-Damascus coolness or lack of
confidence or pride in his race and its unique behests from
God. On the contrary, there are many passages which indicate
that though he had later reached a position where, at least in
moments of passionate exaggeration, he could speak of having
been "in times past in the Jews' religion," he never gave up his
pride in being a Jew or his passionate regard for his fellow
countrymen. Blind though they seemed to him to be, he would
gladly give up his own prized salvation, if that would bring
them to a recognition of God's will (cf. Rom. 9:1-5). Saul, if

so he was named, had a shattering experience—probably, to be more exact, a series of shattering experiences—which led him to reappraise values drastically; but the cause of this was not a lukewarm attitude to the religion of his fathers, which, as a "diaspora Jew," he could easily cast aside.

There was his conversion (to use the term normal for a Christian approaching the story, though one may well doubt that this would be the term Paul would have employed). To see this experience as due to a deep-seated dissatisfaction with the law of Moses and a desire to escape from its bondage into a greater freedom made possible by a God whom he now saw in the face of Jesus, no longer as a stern lawgiver, but as a re-deeming Father; to conclude that like Luther he found no peace in the most exact ritual correctness—all this, though constantly stressed, appears to me utterly unwarranted. There is the oft-quoted and as regularly misunderstood passage in Rom. ch. 7, in which the contrast is made between "the good which I would but cannot, and the evil which I would not do but do," culminating in the tragic outburst:

> Wretched man that I am! who shall deliver me out of the body of this death? I thank God through Jesus Christ our Lord. So then I of myself with the mind, indeed, serve the law of God; but with the flesh the law of sin. (Rom. 7:24-25.)

To see this page as autobiographical and a haunting night-mare memory of Paul's pre-Damascus days is surely unsound. This is not autobiography at all. Rather, it is a paradigm of the condition in which Paul (many years later) now sees every man to be standing, while apart from God and his gracious gift. Surely we have learned enough of that contemporary style of paraenetic address dubbed the "diatribe" [14] to remember that it was common practice to throw the argument into the first person in a far from autobiographical intent. It throws no light whatever on Paul's pre-Damascus days, and to use it as evidence of Paul's indifference or long-developed hostility to the law of Moses is simply perverse. The Paul whom we know from his extant epistles is far removed from the one to whom he looked back with regret. In a word—and a highly important word it is!—Paul was not converted to Paulinism. The Paul we know had moved a long way from the zealous protagonist who had suddenly been forced to recognize that he had been terribly wrong.

At some time in the early years of the Christian beginnings Paul makes his appearance. The probable date has been long debated, due to the artificial story or picture given in Acts: his part in the stoning of Stephen and his subsequent trip to Damascus. All this has seemed to suggest a comparatively early date. Some have even toyed with the possibility that he had himself seen and heard Jesus, perhaps during the days when he sat at the feet of Gamaliel. Thus a date of A.D. 30-32 for his appearance in the Christian story has been suggested. Freed from the Lukan reconstruction, which, as already argued, appears to me a far from secure building stone, a somewhat later date would seem more probable. The movement has spread. It has reached Damascus. To me, the most probable date is ca. A.D. 40. I feel that we will wisely consider the incident mentioned in II Cor. 12:1-6 a very probable clue. That this traumatic experience, in which the man was "caught up even to the third heaven" and heard "unspeakable words, which it is not lawful for a man to utter," was Paul's own needs no argument and has long been conceded by almost all scholars. Nor is this any modern identification. That the "man" referred to was the apostle himself was the regular understanding of all early readers, and the *Apocalypse of Paul* and the so-called *Ascent of Paul* are but two early attempts to set forth in detail the experiences here only hinted at.

I am definitely inclined to consider that this shattering experience, still so vivid before his eyes that he remembers the precise date, "fourteen years ago," was his conversion experience. This has been occasionally suggested but more frequently denied. To me it seems highly probable. That Paul may well have had other moments of ecstasy, made possible by a malady to which he seemingly refers as a "thorn in the flesh" (II Cor. 12:7) and which, from its mention in Galatians (ch. 4:13-14), is not improbably to be diagnosed as epilepsy, would seem to me highly likely. That any of these traumatic experiences was of a sort to eclipse his first encounter, when God saw fit to reveal his Son and to endow him with his message (Gal. 1:15 f.; cf. I Cor. 9:1; 15:8), I should seriously question. The common disinclination on the part of contemporary scholars so to regard this passage is, it appears to me, due to the chronological difficulties seemingly involved—to which matter we will presently turn. If this is sound reasoning, we have here a very definite indication of date. On quite other grounds the date of the so-called "severe letter" (II Cor., chs. 10 to 13), in which this experience is graphically recalled, may be set with reasonable confidence as ca. A.D. 54. "Fourteen years ago" would suggest A.D. 40.

The chronology of Galatians is much less clear-cut; at least it is of a nature to permit of many variations. The statement, "Then after the space of fourteen years I went up again to Jerusalem" (Gal. 2:1), would not seem easily fitted into the chronology suggested in my preceding paragraph, especially if the "fourteen years" is to be added to the previous "after three years," mentioned a few verses before (Gal. 1:18). It is largely because of this seeming impasse that so early a date for Paul's conversion has been suggested. However, as has been occasionally suggested, the difficulty is not impassable. Presumably "fourteen," as written by his scribe, would not be spelled out but indicated by the letters *ID*. When the whole phrase *DIAIDETŌN* (*DIA ID ETŌN*, "after 14 years") is examined, it is seen that everything hinges on the single-stroke letter iota (*I*) in the easily confused unspaced combination *DIAID*.[15] Were that second iota to be regarded as an accidental dittograph, "fourteen" would be reduced to "four." And it is to be noted that, even were the numeral to be spelled out, a similar possibility of primitive scribal error is to be seen, for

DIADEKATESSARŌN (*DIA DEKATESSARŌN* . . . , "after fourteen . . .") would easily allow the initial *DEKA* to be a careless dittograph for *DIA*. It must be frankly recognized that this is conjecture. There is no manuscript known to me giving this reading. Nonetheless, though I am very cautious about employing conjectural emendations, it does not seem in this case utterly reckless. Actually, a *D* ("4") or *TES-SARŌN* ("four") can easily have been changed deliberately by an early copyist to *ID* or *DEKATESSARŌN* to harmonize with II Cor. 12:2.

If this conjecture be allowed, many difficulties vanish. It has been felt that seventeen—even fourteen—years is a very long time of silence for Paul's work in Syria and Cilicia. If, however, instead of fourteen years we have four years, matters would at once straighten out. The two mentioned periods, three years and four years, presumably consecutive, not both "after" the same event, would amount to seven or (allowing for a variation in the reckoning of years) even six. And such a time after A.D. 40 would bring us to approximately A.D. 46-47. To those who do not share my unwillingness to use the stories in Acts as data for definite conclusions, this date A.D. 46-47 may well seem the most probable time for dating the famine which Jerusalem suffered "in the days of Claudius," [16] at which time Paul is said by Acts to have gone to Jerusalem. Presumably the two visits of Paul to Jerusalem mentioned in Acts[17] are to be seen as variant stories—the one from the traditions of Antioch, the other from those of Jerusalem—of the one visit, namely, the one to which Paul is referring in Gal., ch. 2. Thus I incline, although fully aware of the speculative and fragile nature of this suggestion, to postulate A.D. 40 as the most likely date for Paul's change of face.

Prior to his conversion Paul had been engaged in attempting to "persecute the church of God." Presumably this had been done in Damascus. There is no slightest indication in the sober and seemingly factual account in Gal., ch. 1, of any prior activity in Jerusalem or elsewhere or that his shattering experience occurred en route to that city. Were it not for the accounts in Acts, which I have suggested are most likely to be seen as the result of Luke's own rewriting these clues from Paul, it is safe to say that no one would ever have detected any lacunae in Paul's own account.

In the course of his fruitless attempt to "make havoc" of the church of God he had become convinced of his folly. As I have already stressed, it seems to me unwise to understand this change as due to dissatisfaction with Torah or his status as a loyal Jew. Rather, he had become convinced that his opponents were right in their contention that God was blessing them as they sought to do his will. For Paul, and for many other Jews, as he was later to discover to his pain, the cross was a stumbling block (I Cor. 1:23). And small wonder. Did not Deuteronomy say explicitly (Deut. 21:23), as Paul was to paraphrase it, "Cursed is every one that hangeth on a tree" (Gal. 3:13)? Here at base was the ground for Paul's own hostility, the hostility of a passionate Jew who sought to continue "in all things that are written in the book of the law" (Gal. 3:10), not the whimsy of some lukewarm "diaspora Jew" who was indulging for reasons best known to himself in running amok.

What it was that convinced him that they were right—or, as it appears to me he would have phrased it, that God was blessing their endeavors—Paul has not told us. To me the most probable explanation was the manifest success, despite persecution, of the movement. It was growing, and at a startling rate. But there is another factor to be considered. Despite himself, he found himself approving; else the easy answer: "The wicked spread themselves as the green bay tree" (Ps. 37:35). Were I to guess—and most "scholarly hypotheses" might well be so phrased—it would be that he was convinced that he had been terribly wrong, because of what was becoming so evident to his unwilling eyes: the quality of their life and the way they met and overcame his and his fellows' attacks. The real Paul, as revealed in his letters, is the clear-eyed and demanding teacher of ethics, ever mindful of and insistent upon solid qualities of life, not the teacher of an, at best, subjective theology. Thus I am inclined to believe that it was the quality of life which he found himself forced to approve in his opponents which eventually led to his surrender. God was—must be!—blessing them; only so could their success be accounted for.

The next step was inevitable for a Jew who had drawn in with his mother's milk the confidence that God changeth not. If God was blessing the movement, as so obviously he was, he must always so have intended. How, then, could he have cursed Jesus, as the tragedy of the cross seemed to indicate? Manifestly, this could not be. Despite Deuteronomy's ominous word, God had not cursed but blessed Jesus, *despite* the fact that he had been crucified. To me this appears to have been the first step that Paul took and the first conviction that he reached. We know him from his letters, written many years later. In them, as we shall see, many more steps have been taken—some willingly, others forced upon him. Perhaps the most important—at least, for good or ill, it has so appeared— was the change of *despite* to *because*: God has blessed Jesus *because* he was crucified. But this was scarcely his view in these early days. In a word, to repeat an earlier phrase, Paul was not converted to Paulinism.

From persecutor he changed, seemingly overnight, into champion. The adverb *perissoterōs*, translated "more abundantly," "more exceedingly," and frequent in his letters,[18] is one not unnaturally dear to him, for it so completely describes him: what he did, he did with his might. That his change of front—from persecutor to champion—may well have had its traumatic moments appears to me most likely. His growing uncertainty, his attempts to stifle the fear that he was wrong, his growing dread that his opponents, not he, were actually succeeding in what he so passionately had believed he himself was doing, namely, God's service, may well have resulted in an experience in which he was "caught up into the third heaven," "saw Jesus," heard God's voice. In this growing insecurity and unrest, stories which he had heard and sought to reject (e.g., that to chosen followers the crucified Jesus had appeared—a proof of the validity of their claim that far from cursing, God was blessing) may easily have contributed their share to his disquiet and have led to his confidence that to him too had come a similar revelation: "and last of all, as to the child untimely born, he appeared to me also" (I Cor. 15:8). What he has recorded of his ability to speak in tongues, to see visions, to have received God's word directly, with no intermediary—all this would certainly suggest a mental balance that could permit, after a nerve-racking turmoil of indecision, a decisive, if traumatic, experience.

The point of concern is that his resultant message was in all likelihood precisely that of those he had fruitlessly sought to suppress: Jesus, as God's prophet, had sounded forth the speedy dawn of the new age, the coming kingdom; nay, more: he was destined himself to inaugurate it when, in God's good time, it was to dawn. In the interim he was with God in heaven, whither God had taken him. At any moment he would descend again to consummate what he had begun. In this confidence—which, I am convinced, despite many modern efforts to change it drastically, was the earliest kerygma—it is to be noted, there was absolutely no element of hostility to the Mosaic law, no thought of its being a burden now to be laid aside. By God's grace he had been enabled to see that he had been wrong. God had blessed Jesus despite the sinister word anent the cross. Now that he, Paul, knew this—for God had told it to him; had shown him the crucified but resurrected Jesus!—of course his fellow Jews would see it too, once he could speak to them. With this confidence—the confidence of every Semitic prophet, be he a Micaiah, an Amos, a Jeremiah, a Jesus, or a Mohammed—in this role which Paul so certainly took as a result of his shattering encounter in Damascus, we see again the passionate and devoted Jew, to whom the prophetic tradition was an open book; we do not see an indifferent "diaspora Jew." Paul started his mission to his fellow Jews with perfect confidence that as the scales had fallen from his eyes, so they would fall from the eyes of his compatriots.

That Paul believed himself to be, and claimed to be, in the succession of the prophets is at best uncertain, possibly unlikely, although his confidence that his message had been bestowed upon him "not from men, neither through man" (Gal. 1:1), but supernaturally by God himself, so that when he spoke God was actually speaking, raises questions at this point not easily answered and surely not to be overlooked or dismissed lightly. His self-conceded ability to speak in tongues ("I thank God, I speak with tongues more than you all"—I Cor. 14:18) would surely suggest a temperament far from alien to those who could so regard themselves. The confidence, often expressed in his letters, appears most unmistakably in his outraged word to the Galatians:

> But though we, or an angel from heaven, should preach unto you any gospel other than that which we preached unto you, let him be anathema. As we have said before, so say I now again, If any man preacheth unto you any gospel other than that which ye received, let him be anathema. (Gal. 1:8-9.)

This is of a piece with the confidence of all the prophets of Israel, be it a Micaiah ("As Yahweh liveth, what Yahweh saith unto me, that will I speak"—I Kings 22:14), or a Jeremiah ("The word of Yahweh came unto me, saying . . ."—Jer. 32:6), or a Jesus ("Ye have heard that it was said to them of old time . . . but I say unto you . . ."—Matt. 5:21 f.). Words which can easily seem unwarranted arrogance must be differently assessed in this setting, so remote and alien to modern men. As Paul so phrases himself, it is not the arrogant stating of his own views; it is, rather, the faithful and obedient announcement of the word of the Almighty, who, in his own unfathomable judgment, has chosen him as his mouthpiece.

There may well be the opportunity for pondering the mental adjustment of any man, be he a Micaiah, an Amos, a Jeremiah, a Jesus, or a Paul, that permits him to reach this conclusion so basic to the Semitic prophet; there can be no question of the "that," although a wide possibility of diagnosis may well be left open in attempting to answer the "why" and the "how."

The canonical Scriptures—God's all-inclusive revelation—had come to be regarded as the way he communicated with men. Thus in popular thought and phrase, since the holy spirit was specifically the spirit of prophecy—"all the prophets spake by the holy spirit"—when Haggai, Zechariah, and Malachi, the last of the prophets, died, the holy spirit departed from Israel.[19] But nonetheless, none other than Moses himself had made mention of the coming of a prophet "like unto me" (Deut. 18:15, 18). Nor was this word forgotten. Not only do we find occasional references to this long-expected prophet, in words in the mouth of a Judas Maccabeus (I Macc. 4:44-47) or the Samaritan woman (John 4:19), but it is impossible to read with understanding the Synoptic Gospels without seeing the emphasis, constant though deliberately lessened, suggesting that not only did his hearers regard Jesus as a prophet but that in all probability this identification of him as such was due to his own confidently uttered claim to be God's prophet, not improbably *the* prophet "like unto Moses." Thus the possibility that Paul too may have toyed with such a notion is not to be dismissed as impossible or even unlikely. Remember his words descriptive of God's call to him—

> But when it was the good pleasure of God, who separated me, even from my mother's womb, and called me through his grace, to reveal his Son in me, that I might preach him among the Gentiles (Gal. 1:15-16),

and compare Jeremiah's corresponding word—

> Now the word of Yahweh came unto me saying, Before I formed thee in the belly I knew thee, and before thou camest

forth out of the womb I sanctified thee; I have appointed thee
a prophet unto the nations (Jer. 1:4, 5).

It is not easy to deny that Paul's phrasing is very certainly
affected by Jeremiah's or that Paul saw himself in a position
definitely akin to that of his great predecessor.

The Paul we find in his letters is a determined apostle to the
Gentiles, with a message in which law and gospel are ar-
raigned against one another, and in which "Christ crucified" is
central. That at the time he was writing these letters he was
convinced that in all this there was no change, but that it was
the compelling intent of God when he called him, is certain.
Nonetheless, although Paul could not have been expected to
see it, there may well have been an interim chapter highly important for a correct understanding of him.

It is most unlikely that, at the time of Paul's change from
opponent to champion, the death of Jesus on the cross had
come to be regarded as planned and ordained by God as the
mysterium tremendum theologicum, or that Jesus' death was
regarded "a ransom for many," as it was later to be phrased
(Mark 10:45; Matt. 20:28), the way God was seeking to reconcile the world to himself (II Cor. 5:19). Rather, it was a hor-
rid crime, but one more example of blindness on the part of
these misguided fellow Jews: "As your fathers killed the
prophets, so do ye." This note, so central in the early
preaching as revealed in Acts (Acts 7:51 ff.; cf. 2:23; 3:17 ff.;
5:30), seems primitive and of a sort to raise definite questions
as to the legitimacy of much modern confident reconstruction
of the "earliest kerygma."

Presumably the "stumbling block of the cross" was as real a
one to the early protagonists as it was to their opponents. To
me, the most marked indication of the almost magnetic power
Jesus seems to have exerted over many of his hearers, who
were convinced that his claim to be God's prophet sent to
them to announce the near approach of the long-looked-for
kingdom was true, was that his tragic death did not destroy

that confidence, but instead that in the eyes of many it was easier to disbelieve—or to explain away—the seeming verdict of the cross than to believe that Jesus had been mistaken. It was this deathless confidence which led to the confident claims that they had seen their triumphant Lord. Mark and his followers, eagerly espoused by the theologians, inverted these steps, with their picture of the utter breakdown in morale, even of the most immediate followers, changed by God's intervention and miraculous restoration of a battered body. In a word, as champions of this emphasis would have it, the chief concern is not the Sermon on the Mount but the Cross on the Hill. Thus the Jesus of history has been allowed to fade away into but a vague shadow. To me this is far from convincing. Far more likely, it appears to me, is the essential reverse. The impress the imperious prophet had made, their confidence that he had been sent and was blessed by God, made it impossible for them that Jesus either had deluded them or had himself been deluded. He must have triumphed; he himself must speedily return to accomplish what they now believed he had meant in his enigmatic references to the misunderstood "Son of man."

To some, the "stumbling block of the cross" yielded to this deathless confidence—and we owe what we now know as Christianity in no small measure to that dauntless faith. But for many, probably many who had hearkened and thrilled when the prophet was in their midst, the confidence faded: "We had hoped . . ." To others, who had been either hostile or indifferent, the ignominious death was the perfect proof of the absurdity of his claims and of his followers' confident repetition. The undaunted insistence of his followers that he had been sent by God, blessed by God, uniquely honored by God, was not only nonsense but blasphemy. Moses had stated without qualification that those who died by this form of death were under God's curse. God, not the Sanhedrin or Pontius Pilate, was in control. That he had permitted the act—and else it could not have occurred—was clear.

To challenge this, as these riffraff preachers were doing, was grave sin. To be sure, in most other respects they were good Jews. They observed the proper ways of life, were sound in what were the fundamentals of religion: the unity of God, his relation to Israel, his complete revelation in Scripture. Their belief in resurrection, which speedily became a foundation stone in the growing movement, was of little moment. This had long been adopted by the Pharisees. Their confidence that the end of the age was near, to be ushered in with apocalyptic rumblings, was far from unique to them. Their notion that their leader was to be instrumental in this coming last chapter was eccentric, perhaps absurd, but there was no sacrosanct "doctrine of the Messiah" that alone could be considered orthodox. That they had queer notions of being uniquely inspired by the Spirit, that they were making converts, that due to their confidence that the end was momentarily to come they were pooling their resources, sharing what they had, and making no provision for the future ("You can't take it with you") —all of this might make the group seem queer, perhaps annoying; but there was nothing really vicious. But the fact that the one to whom they were were giving such honors had died by a form of death which Torah showed was proof of God's displeasure and curse: that did make a difference. The claim that one who, according to Torah, was under God's curse was instead enjoying God's blessing—that was different. That was a stumbling block. That did lead, at least occasionally, to reprisal.

In consequence of his shattering experience Paul found himself over this stumbling block which had been the spur to his opposition. Thus it is probable that in his new confidence Paul expected to be able to convince his fellow Jews that "despite the cross"—not "because of it"—Jesus had been blessed by God and as his agent would speedily return to consummate what he had earlier proclaimed: in a word, that his followers, Paul's erstwhile opponents, were right in their claim.

Of course his fellow Jews would hear, would see, the truth

even as he did: such has always been the first confidence of
the prophet. But they did not see, would not hear. Why?
Something must be holding them back, blinding their eyes.
Whatever that something was, it must be evil, for otherwise
they would hearken to God's voice, even as he had. What was
the fatal obstacle? Jesus, in not unlike perplexity, had found
the obstacles to be wealth and education: the wealthy and the
learned were turning a deaf ear to what Jesus *knew* was God's
word; the poor were eagerly hearkening and obeying. Thus
the answer seems clear and accounts, without sociological
analysis, for his marked opposition to wealth and his confidence in the "little ones" still so evident in the Gospels.

For Paul the same question, Why? was central, and for Paul
the answer was clear. It was the death on the cross which was
proving to be for his hearers, as for a long time it had proved
to be for him, the fatal obstacle. This proved that God's blessing could not rest on what was so signally an object of his displeasure. Seeing this problem, realizing that here was the real
crux—and being the sort of man that he was—he refused to
yield, refused to seek an easier or more defensible avenue of
approach. General Grant declared before Richmond, "I'll fight
it out on this line if it takes all summer!" Similarly, Paul declared what his message was to be: "Jesus Christ and him
crucified." In the course of the years, first (presumably) in
fruitless attempts to batter down Jewish prejudice, later, when
that proved futile, in his turn to the Gentiles, his constant
stress upon the one central problem led to his discovering in it
ever-widening implications. In a word, again to abbreviate
drastically, the word "despite" came to yield to the very different "because of." But this change did not take place overnight, and apparently it was not the consequence of an
immediate "turning to the Gentiles." The Jews' inability to see,
and their not unnatural hostility to Paul, whom they considered a turncoat and traitor (to the prophet, hostility to himself
always is hostility to God)—these led to Paul's radical reap-
praisal and resulted in his seemingly more satisfying explana-

tion of the cross. For Paul, now, the cross was not man's act, out of blind opposition; rather, in the cross God had acted—using, as he so often did, man's folly for his own purposes.

Another consequence must not be overlooked. The all-important and all-tragic source of Jewish obtuseness, in the eyes of Paul, was not the Jews' hostility to God. It was not hostility to God, any more than his own earlier opposition had been. They loved God as devotedly as did he. What then could be holding them back? And the answer seemed all too clear: it was the sinister word of Moses, which had earlier lent confidence to Paul's own opposition. Again, in a word, it was the Law. The Law could not be correct in its appraisal, for it stood so clearly in stark opposition to what God himself had revealed to him. Paul reached this conclusion in consequence of long and fruitless attempts to meet the issue, to fight the battle on this so-critical front (which surely he never dreamed of when he first became convinced of his tragic, if innocent, alignment against God and his chosen Son): law *vs.* gospel. It was not dissatisfaction with the Law, or growing restiveness under its constraints that had gradually led an "insecure" Jew to break away from his traditional past and to free himself easily from what should have spelled freedom. Rather, he broke away because in the Law was to be found the fatal obstacle which deafened the ears to God's so insistent demands.

Eventually Paul turned to the Gentiles, not because he was a lukewarm, Hellenized Jew seeking a naturally more congenial clime, but, apparently—as had been the case earlier with other protagonists—because of the increasing opposition and the hopelessness of success among his fellow Jews. How far did Paul go? To him it was a great way. Certainly that is a far from unique situation. To every convert, if the decision is more than skin-deep, the answer is always the same: "Whereas I was blind, now I see." More than that, the breaking of old ties, always a continued source of pain, and the resultant sadness and loneliness may well heighten the actual distance of departure.

Did his Gentile hearers feel the same? Did they see him as he now saw himself? Certainly indications in such letters as I Corinthians and Galatians would suggest quite the reverse. These letters suggest that to many in Galatia he appeared to be a Jew, who, despite his claims, was seeking to force upon them needless and unwarranted restraints. His insistence that, though freed from the requirements of the Mosaic law, they were yet subject to precisely the same demands because such alone were "worthy of one in Christ" seemed to them, as it did to many in Corinth, and presumably in all his other Gentile churches, simple casuistry. "To the Jews I became as a Jew, that I might gain Jews; to them that are under the law, as under the law . . ." (I Cor. 9:20-21) may well be pondered. Paul might continue, "not being myself under the law, that I might gain them that are under the law," but to Gentiles—such as Paul very definitely was not—this qualification may well have seemed meaningless.

It is certainly possible that the somewhat awkwardly obscure wording of Gal. 2:3 ff. indicates that Titus, Gentile though he was, was circumcised, though not "under compulsion." (Naturally, the circumcision of Timothy in Acts 16:3 without confirmation from Paul's own pen is not available as evidence.) If Gal. 2:3 ff. indeed so indicates, we can see a background which made natural the charge that, despite his brave words, Paul was, at least on occasion, "preaching circumcision." Certainly, his heated denial—"But I, brethren, if I still preach circumcision, why am I still persecuted?" (Gal. 5:11)—can only be understood as an answer to those who were charging him with so doing, not to those to whom such an act must have seemed praiseworthy.

Nor should this patent fact be overlooked: despite Paul's much touted "break with the Law," he gave a fundamental place to ethics, especially to sexual ethics; precisely the qualities which he insisted were alone worthy of one who was in Christ—these were the qualities demanded by the Law. Here is a matter to be weighed very carefully by those who are inclined too easily to reach conclusions, in part from Phil., ch. 3, in part from surmises about the obvious endowment—or lack of it—of a halfway Jew who grew up far from Zion and its devotion to the ancestral ways and beliefs.

Again it is easy—but most unwarranted, if we are to hope to view the man correctly—to overlook his obvious and sustained feeling of the superiority of Jew to Gentile. His stress upon broken-down walls of separation seems clear and unqualified: "There can be neither Jew nor Greek, there can be neither bond nor free, there can be no male and female; for ye are all one in Christ Jesus" (Gal. 3:28). Ideally, yes—in the eyes of God. But while a path of access for all stood open, had been opened at infinite cost, and stood open for all equally, this equality in the eyes of God was far from synonymous with complete equality in very human eyes; despite a modern attempt to turn Paul, like Jesus before him, into a universalist for whom no differences or personal preferences still obtained. That Paul actually felt that male and female—whatever the verdict of God—were equal in dignity and status would appear to me, in view of his very definitely expressed words, a position hard to maintain (I Cor. 14:34 ff.; cf. I Cor. 11:2-16). The same may be said with some confidence of master and slave. A bit of realism, even of common sense, may well be exercised in our understanding of his theology and his often distinctly different personal opinions—both alike known to us from their chance appearance in letters intended to correct abuses, not from their deliberate inclusion in a studied epitome or compendium of Christian theology.

"What advantage then hath the Jew? or what is the profit of circumcision?" Paul's answer is clear and may well be pondered: "Much every way" (Rom. 3:1 f.). This answer seems startlingly in contrast to what we might have expected from his immediately preceding words. Nor is there any satisfactory or persuasive argument to justify this amazing apparent *non sequitur*. He drops the subject to resume it in chs. 9 to 11 with the reason for his so-strong affirmative. But one thing is very

clear: in this terse affirmative, which needs no buttressing, a
Jew, not a Greek, is speaking. And, as we read his letters as
coming from an apostle to the Gentiles, we need not limit our
quest to rhetorical questions of a sort to allow uncertain conclusions. The passing, but sobering, word expressing horror at
the case of flagrant immorality in the church at Corinth and,
even worse, the lack of concern, the almost smug compla-
cence, that others in the congregation are showing with regard
to the awful act of the errant brother (". . . there is fornication among you, and such fornication *as is not even among the
Gentiles*"—I Cor. 5:1) reveals the man with his theological
guard down. Paul has become, at least in his own eyes, an
"apostle to the Gentiles," and can easily read this commission
back to the very moment when God had first made known his
long-held intent (Gal. 1:15-16); but not only had the role
been forced upon him, it was a heavy load and a constant
source of horror. Reference is frequent in his letters to the
murky and miasmal condition from which Gentiles had
emerged into the sunshine of the gospel; this finds its complet-
est and most revealing indictment in the last half of the first
chapter of Romans (Rom. 1:18-32). Here most certainly a
Jew of unimpaired Jewishness is speaking, aghast at the laxity
in sexual ethics which he found wherever he went as he continued his mission year in, year out. Certainly his years in
Tarsus, if such be imagined, had not noticeably lessened his
ancestral heritage in this regard.

Regularly Paul's lists of vices start with those of a sexual
nature. A careful examination of how he treats this matter—
what he does say, and what he does not—is very revealing. It
shows Paul entirely free from the almost morbid fascination
which later successors (notably, but not limited to, Jerome
and Epiphanius) show in dilating and calling attention to details which the virgins to whom they are writing are to be sure
not to look at too closely. All of this, unfortunately so natural
as a consequence of asceticism (nature seemingly objects to
too disparate cutting across her pattern of life), is quite absent

in Paul. He warns as he does solely because brothers for whom Christ died are in deadly peril if they fall victim. Basically, Paul is a thoroughly honest and clean-minded man. He can give body blows, but they are never for effect or to permit him to expand upon what he only pretended to detest.

Here a concluding word is in order: When we read Phil. 3:2-11 and the equally extreme statements in his tear-blotted letter to the "foolish Galatians" (words that were colored by Paul's extreme emotion of the moment and subsequently drastically recast by him), they should not blind our eyes to the word of Paul, rich in pathos and honest pride of heritage: "Did God cast off his people? God forbid. For I also am an Israelite, of the seed of Abraham, of the tribe of Benjamin." (Rom. 11:1.) The never-to-be-forgotten word—when we seek rightly to appraise this stormy petrel of the yester-years—is found in the opening paragraph of Rom., chs. 9 to 11. This section bristles with difficulties and is replete with (to us) most unsatisfactory and labored argument. But this opening word is perfectly clear:

> I say the truth in Christ, I lie not, my conscience bearing witness with me in the Holy Spirit, that I have great sorrow and unceasing pain in my heart. For I could wish that I myself were anathema from Christ for my brethren's sake, my kinsmen according to the flesh: who are Israelites; whose is the adoption, and the glory, and the covenants, and the giving of the law, and the service of God, and the promises; whose are the fathers, and of whom is Christ as concerning the flesh, who is over all, God blessed for ever. Amen. (Rom. 9:1-5.)

Here in this letter—in my judgment the last we have from his pen, most certainly his "last will and testament" to his several churches, now that he is turning to the far West—we see Paul the clearest.[20] Many of his earlier words in others letters, written at times in fury and not corrected with phlegm, stand here, repeated but without the exaggerations and overemphases called forth in the midst of debate from one intent to win his case.

In the course of Paul's years of missionary service in the larger Mediterranean world, to men and women whose ways of life he disapproved and whom he found repugnant in the extreme (but the hand of God was upon him, driving him to the task, for they too were "brothers [and sisters] for whom Christ had died"), the gospel he had received in Damascus came to be greatly changed. Paul, of course, was completely unaware of the change as he looked back on his experience of freedom since he had become Christ's slave. The task of translating it, not alone its language but its content, to make it intelligible to his hearers—this led him to changes and developments that can be neither overlooked nor minimized. To many, some of the new notes that appeared were unfortunate, and many of the elements which gradually dropped from the picture were amazing if not almost unforgivable; nonetheless, quite regardless of the place of his birth and the nature of his early education, one thing is very clear: to his dying day Paul could say—and did!—with undiminished pride: "I . . . *am* an Israelite, of the seed of Abraham," not "I *was* . . ." [21]

5 | STRAIGHTWAY

"I went away into Arabia"

To attempt a biography or life of Paul, save in the vaguest and most general terms, is manifestly absurd. His letters, our one sure source of information, are far from providing many of what can be called exact chronographic hints. On the other hand, the letters themselves, for the most part indicating the recipients, give a clear picture, or series of pictures, of places and people with whom he had intimate contacts in the form of extended visits, during a period of a decade and a half or a bit longer. And occasionally in the letters chance words or allusions will aid in a cautious attempt to order these obscure years of service.

As we have seen, the mention of Damascus as the place where, years before, he had changed from persecutor to champion gives us a seemingly secure foundation stone. If my contention that his allusion to a moment of ecstasy "fourteen years ago" is a reference to the conversion, and if the suggested date, ca. A.D. 54 for the composition of the letter which mentions this experience, be accepted, we can hazard the guess that ca. A.D. 40 is, as has been remarked, a likely date for this right-about-face.

The account in Galatians continues:

. . . straightway I conferred not with flesh and blood: neither went I up to Jerusalem to them that were apostles before me:

but I went away into Arabia; and again I returned unto
Damascus. Then after three years I went up to Jerusalem to
visit Cephas, and tarried with him fifteen days. (Gal. 1:16-18.)

It might seem at first reading that we have here a definitely
dated outline of events, even if tersely drawn. But the more
they are studied, the more elusive the words become. "I went
away into Arabia" is far from clear, but is almost hopelessly
obscured by the interlocked companion queries, Where? and
Why? "Arabia" is a very vague term and of the sort to pique
conjecture. The answer to the companion query, Why? has
seemed to many investigators obvious: to meditate in the
desert. As Moses had hastened to Sinai (Ex. 19:3; 24:9 ff.,
15-18), as Elijah, too, fled to Horeb (= Sinai?) (I Kings 19:1-
8), so Paul, after his equally cataclysmic experience, sought
solitude, not improbably on the holy mountain. Certainly this
reading into the text is not impossible, and it provides a satisfactory explanation to those who wish to see Paul, if not converted to Paulinism, at least attaining his basic gospel with the
least delay. Actually it is at precisely that point that I find this
explanation unlikely. Far more of an obstacle to this solution
than the rugged four-hundred-mile trek to the fabled mountain is the fancied need so easily imagined of straightening his
thinking out. To me there was nothing needing straightening
out as Paul saw it. He had been wrong; God had made this
clear to him. The obstacle—God's seeming curse upon Jesus
and his mission—had been removed. God had appointed him,
Paul, his special prophet to aid his fellows to see the truth as
he now did. Not yet had he been confronted with a Jewry
deaf to his (i.e., God's) revealing word. Later, when Jewish
opposition had both forced him to theological conclusions
which at the moment he never dreamed of and had made the
Gentiles, not the Jews, his field of endeavor, he could, of
course, easily and honestly read all this back to the all-
important instant when the scales had fallen from his eyes. But
that this had been realized at the moment he went into Ara-

bia seems to me most unlikely. Not that he was not eager to preach what now he was sure was true; but was Arabia a likely place to find Jews whom he might rescue from their blindness? It would seem that Paul, the missioner to the Gentiles, strategically sought the important cities of the Roman East—Antioch, Ephesus, Philippi, Thessalonica, Athens, Corinth—as workshops. This at-homeness in cities may well have been no new and acquired touch: Damascus, where he is first found, was a city large and prominent. Thus if the purpose of his expedition to Arabia was, as is certainly far from impossible, to get to work without delay, such cities as Bostra and Petra might have been his goal. But the problem remains. If Paul had already seen his mission to the Gentiles, an Arabian mission would be natural. If not, would it not have been far more natural for his first attempts to have been in Damascus, where Jews, who needed his insight, were to be found?

Thus I find both of the common explanations of the (by him) unexplained sudden departure to Arabia unconvincing. There is a third alternative, but it has, as far as I can see, rarely or never been suggested: to escape arrest or even death. A possible clue to this is available to us, but apparently it was equally available to Luke, whose rewriting of the incident has led modern investigators astray. They have been content to correct Luke's account of the nature of the peril Paul faced, and have failed to see the probable incorrectness of the time when this danger was so dramatically escaped.

Paul cites the incident as but one of the many perils he had undergone:

> In Damascus the ethnarch under Aretas the king guarded the city of the Damascenes in order to take me: and through a window was I let down in a basket by the wall, and escaped his hands. (II Cor. 11:32-33.)

Luke utilizes this brief account as the reason which led Paul to make the trip to Jerusalem, to which Paul himself subsequently refers:

And when many days were fulfilled, the Jews took counsel together to kill him: but their plot became known to Saul. And they watched the gates also day and night that they might kill him: but his disciples took him by night, and let him down through the wall, lowering him in a basket. (Acts 9:23-25.)

In Paul's account it was to escape "the ethnarch under Aretas the king" (outside the walls?) that he fled. As Luke retells it, it was to escape the murderous rage of the Jews within the city. That Luke's account is secondary surely needs no argument. It would certainly have been a strange procedure for Paul, having already incurred Jewish wrath in Damascus, to have fled, of all places, to Jerusalem. But this emphasis is one which Luke makes again and again. Regularly he seeks to free Paul, and other Christians as well, from the suspicion of having incurred official displeasure. It is always the Jews who have hampered and hindered.

Most modern critics would, I think, agree substantially that Luke's account is secondary, but would assume his knowledge of the incident to have come from some sort of tradition known to him. Failing to consider the possibility that Luke's source of knowledge was the Pauline word, they have tacitly dated the episode at the end of the postconversion days in Damascus, as seemingly guaranteed by this imaginary tradition. If, as would seem to me more probable, there was no other tradition known to Luke, but that he read the word in II Corinthians as we do, and utilized it, at once the possibility is seen that this flight was not to Jerusalem, at the end of the three years, but to Arabia at the start of them.

And on this assumption many difficulties would vanish. As soon as he had changed from persecutor to champion Paul had sought, with seemingly little or no success, to enlighten his fellow Jews in Damascus. Not only had they "failed to see," but their hostility to Paul, whom they not unnaturally considered a turncoat and traitor, had been aroused. Thus he had speedily come to be regarded as a troublemaker. That Aretas ever held Damascus in the days of the empire is most unlikely. It has been assumed, as we have mentioned earlier, largely on the basis of this passage, and because no imperial coins have been found in Damascus bearing the impress of Caius or Claudius, that at the death of Tiberius in A.D. 37 Damascus had been removed from the province of Syria and transferred to Aretas. But this is an argument from silence writ large. It would appear to me far more probable that this ethnarch of Aretas was essentially the head of the Nabatean residents in Damascus, responsible for their control and interests and thus not unlike the Jewish "ethnarch" whom Josephus mentions as governing the people and adjudicating their suits in Alexandria.[22] No one would assume from this reference to this ethnarch that Alexandria belonged to the Jews; so in the mention of Aretas' ethnarch in Damascus, no more is to be seen than a similar provision.

Thus it seems to me more natural to see Paul fleeing Damascus to escape the attention of the authorities now that he had achieved notoriety as a troublemaker than to imagine him traveling into Arabia in search of possible Jewish converts or trekking to Sinai to evolve a theology presumably to be of value in subsequent years. Two minor arguments would seem to strengthen the case for this solution. What led Paul back to Damascus? Was it after a lengthy journey to Sinai? Was it at the conclusion of a ministry in Bostra? Is it not far more likely that it was only a short absence, with a return as soon as safety was assured? Aretas ended his reign in A.D. 40. If, as seems probable, Paul's conversion is to be dated in that year, his fear of Aretas' ethnarch would have been ended in but a few months at the most. Nor is it to be neglected that Paul's reference in II Corinthians to this flight is prefaced by the words, "If I must needs glory, I will glory of the things that concern my weakness" (II Cor. 11:30). Is this an indication that it had been fear that had led to his flight? Is it an evidence of embarrassment at the memory of an act far from his usual practice? Is it in answer to his critics' sneers at the real nature of his bravery? Perhaps the query is trifling. Even

if so, it does not lessen the fact that this is a simple and un-
cumbered explanation of the departure to Arabia and his
speedy return once more to seek among the Jews in Damascus
—and perhaps elsewhere in the province—converts to the
cause of God now so clear to him and demanding his devoted
effort.

6 | THE BROADENING WAY

Extended horizons

"Then after three years I went up to Jerusalem to visit Cephas." (Gal. 1:18.) This is the next in the small, but valued, series of clues available from the letters for our picture of Paul's missionary career. The three years may be understood as subsequent to his return from Arabia; more probably, as it seems to me, subsequent to his conversion. If the conjecture expressed in the preceding chapter is sound, the two would be essentially one, as the stay in Arabia would have been very short. Presumably the interim of two years[23] or less after his return to Damascus was devoted to preaching. Nor is there anything to demand that the whole period, long or short, was spent in Damascus. It is entirely possible that he may even have visited Antioch, less than two hundred miles to the west. Nor does there seem to be in this brief allusion any compelling demand for us to see the trip as leading to Jerusalem from Damascus. We are accustomed so to regard it because of the account in Acts. We customarily assume that the reason for the departure south from Damascus was to escape the hostility he had aroused in that city. All this is at best conjecture. All Paul says is that he went to Jerusalem "to visit Cephas," which would seem to suggest: "to make the acquaintance of." Certainly, as has already been remarked, if this departure is from Damascus and was made to escape Jewish hostility, now fanned to a murderous rage, Jerusalem would seem a strange sort of asylum.

Again the reason for Paul's desire at this time to "become acquainted with Peter" (for certainly Cephas and Peter are simply variants) is far from clear. One thing is certain. Paul made a trip for some reason at this time. All these details are incidental to his passionate insistence that his contacts with Jerusalem and those who had been apostles before him had been minimal and that the charge that his gospel had been given him from them is baseless. Thus, unless he is to be charged with a perversion of facts—and his passionate word, "before God I lie not" (Gal. 1:20), makes this most unlikely— he did not go for the purpose of making his gospel more complete at the hands of those whose call antedated his. The word Paul used to indicate his reason is apparently carefully chosen and deliberately laconic. Apparently the visit, the first he had ever made to Jerusalem, is to be dated ca. A.D. 43.

The visit, whatever its purpose and result, was a short one: apparently he was Peter's house guest for fifteen days. He gives no slightest hint as to what he did during that two-week visit. His one word is a negative: Peter was the only apostle whom he saw, except James. Luke attempts to fill in the very sketchy picture, even at the expense of contradicting or drastically recasting Paul's own words: Paul had sought to join the disciples in Jerusalem but without success; Barnabas had intervened and had taken him to the apostles; Paul had preached boldly in and out of Jerusalem and had disputed with the Hellenists, who sought to kill him, just as those in Damascus had done; the "brethren" had spirited him away to Caesarea, where he had departed (apparently by ship) to Tarsus (Acts 9:26-30). That Luke is here following any other source than Paul's own phrases known to us in Galatians appears to me most unlikely. He has unhesitatingly recast the story: as in Damascus, so in Jerusalem, Paul is rescued by the faithful Christian disciples from the hostile Jews, always the source of hostility to the growing movement.

In his rapid review (in Galatians) of the events following his conversion in Damascus, followed by a hasty and unde-scribed fifteen-day stay with Peter in Jerusalem, Paul continues:

> Then I came into the regions of Syria and Cilicia. And I was still unknown by face unto the churches of Judaea which were in Christ: but they only heard say, He that once persecuted us now preacheth the faith of which he once made havoc; and they glorified God in me. (Gal. 1:21-24.)

Too long we have read this through the eyes of Luke: this lengthy period had been spent in Tarsus, where the disciples in Jerusalem had sent him after his rescue from the hostile non-Christian Jews. Paul's own phrasing (despite Luke's mis-understanding of it), "Then I came into the regions of Syria and Cilicia," suggests a quite different interpretation. Following his visit to Jerusalem Paul had engaged for a period of years—commonly understood as fourteen, but, as I have suggested, not improbably to be limited to four (i.e., A.D. 43-47)—in zealous preaching in what he styled "Syria and Cilicia." This locale would appear to me far from wisely limited to Tarsus. "Syria and Cilicia" suggest a much broader area, including almost certainly Antioch and (at least, eastern) Asia Minor.

Since there is no suggestion that he returned to Damascus, it is at least probable that upon his departure from Jerusalem he had gone north to Antioch, a most natural site for work. Here was a great city with a large Jewish colony. There would seem no reason to suppose that at the start of this period Paul had definitely determined on a course as a wandering, itinerant missionary. He had yet to become convinced that God's imperative call had been in terms of such service. Rather, he was confronted with the task of showing brother Jews the truth that to him now loomed so large. What better spot could be chosen than the great metropolis on the Orontes,

ranking with Alexandria and Rome as one of the three greatest
cities of the Mediterranean world? Here were already many
Jews who had come to see that God had blessed, not cursed,
the prophet whom he had sent as his final revelation. In this
broad-gauged center, free from fanatic opposition, there was a
far more probable hope for success. Naturally, with no information save for occasional touches in his letters, it is idle to attempt to reconstruct this period of work. That it was devoted
to preaching may be assumed without question. His intriguing
word of summary (Gal. 1:21-24, quoted above) would certainly seem to confirm this confidence. We can further assume
that during these years, so intriguing and elusive, a definite
widening of his horizon took place.

The next incident he records—his second trip to Jerusalem
—starts with a revealing word:

> Then after the space of fourteen [four?] years I went up again
> to Jerusalem with Barnabas, taking Titus also with me. And I
> went up by revelation; and I laid before them *the gospel which
> I preach among the Gentiles* . . . (Gal. 2:1-2.)

We have seen that his conversion had been his conviction that
he had been dreadfully wrong in attempting to stay the gospel
preachers. Convinced of his folly, he had without delay
started to "preach the faith of which he had earlier made
havoc." But there is nothing to indicate or make probable that
this preaching was to be addressed to Gentiles. Since in the
lapse of the years this had come to be his mission, it is not surprising that looking back over the years he saw this as the divine plan from the beginning—whatever is done, God doeth it.

We cannot hope to fill in the missing details with any exact-
ness, but their general nature would seem highly probable. He
had been enabled—"forced" is perhaps the better word—over
the obstacle of the cross. His confidence was real that now
that his eyes were opened, now that God's message was on his

lips, others to whom the cross was a forbidding stumbling block would see and gain life as he had. This hope was doomed to failure. Possibly in Damascus, not improbably in Jerusalem, now in his continued preaching in Syria and Cilicia, he was coming to see that his radiant expectation—so often the lot of the prophet—was not to be realized. His brother Jews refused to see what to him was now so clear: God's total revelation was not included in this book from the past, for it said so definitely that God's curse must rest on the Crucified and those who blasphemously proclaimed him. But this was surely wrong. God himself had shown by the miracle of the resurrection that he had uniquely blessed this one who now lived with him in glory, soon to return in even more glorious fulfillment. The resurrected Christ was, at least in part, God's revelation, for surely God had expressly sent him to earth and to death for a definite, all-important purpose.

This would seem to me a not improbable first chapter in what we may style Paul's developing theology. During the next few years in Antioch and its environs it appears to me far from unlikely that Paul found a situation—at first forced upon him—which was drastically to affect his thinking and action. Gentiles, already accustomed to find values in Jewish services of worship, were far more ready to accept this new contention that the crucified but speedily resurrected Jesus had been sent by God as his truly all-important revelation to mankind. For them the obstacle of the cross—the warning word of Moses— was less repellent. To some the cross might be foolishness, but to many others such a tragic death had simply been a meaningful prelude. Many a deity had died only to pass on to his votaries information, to be learned through the "things done" and the "things said," whereby they too would be assured a happy reception in the world beyond the grave, where the triumphant deity now resided:

> Be of good courage, ye initiates, because the god has been saved; to us also shall be salvation from woes.[24]

As truly as Osiris lives, he also shall live; as truly as Osiris is
not dead, shall he not die; as truly as Osiris is not annihilated,
shall he not be annihilated.[25]

With such a background, many a Gentile found attractive and
inviting this early Christian preaching of the glorious age soon
to dawn, to be brought about by the return of God's Son, who
had been sent to earth for this purpose and soon resurrected
by God to glorious triumph. The bare form of the original
message, as proclaimed by the prophet Jesus himself, might
well have fallen on deaf ears in the Gentile world. However,
with the rapid modifications by his devoted followers, who
had come to see in the prophet himself the supernatural figure
destined by God to return in glory to consummate what he
had earlier announced, much of the "foolishness" would re-
treat. The offer would seem most enticing, especially since en-
trance to this mystery was not only far less expensive but
freed from many orgiastic details so conspicuous in some of
the other, similar cults. Thus baptism—the initial rite of purifi-
cation, so natural in its origin as the early Christian preachers
sought to make converts (proselytes) to their form of Judaism
—and the communion meal may well have seemed far from
strange or repulsive to many a Gentile in such places as Antioch and Tarsus, to mention but two of the leading cities of
"Syria and Cilicia." Nor should it be overlooked that Gentile
hearers to whom this sort of material was not uncommon may
well have seen—or thought that they saw—more in the gospel
preaching than the preachers themselves had intended.

If Paul found such to be the consequence of his preaching—
deafness on the part of rigid Jews, interest and acceptance by
many Gentiles—it would be no great wonder if in this circumstance he found the turn in the road not only natural but compelling. Clearly, the Law was not the final revelation of God,
for by its unqualified verdict as to the cross and its failure to
include God's purpose, so clearly revealed in the experience of
his Son, it had been proven beyond doubt to be at least incom-

plete. The resurrection proved beyond doubt that "Cursed is every one who hangeth on a tree" is not God's final word on that subject. If the Law is incomplete or in error on this point, as it so manifestly must be, may it not well be so elsewhere too? May it not be, at least in part, but preliminary to the final and complete—or completing—revelation? Three times the Law sounds the imperative and unqualified demand: "Three times in the year all thy males shall appear before the Lord Yahweh" (Ex. 23:17; 34:23; 16:16). But the dispersion of Jews, far from Zion, not only in the Gentile world but in distant parts of Palestine itself, had long since made this ancient law obsolete.

It would seem improbable that there had been any marked hesitation by the early disciples, even in Jerusalem, to seek to make converts to their form of Judaism. Baptism, which speedily was turned into a sacrament, and which appeared in many Gentile eyes as one of the "things done" in this new mystery cult, had apparently started as proselyte baptism, a severely Jewish rite. Thus we are quite justified in seeing two distinct steps in what may be styled a Gentile ministry: first, the feeling, present from the start, that Gentiles were proper subjects to be preached to; second, that Gentiles may be eaten with. It is easy to treat these two emphases as one, but that they were one is certainly far from probable. Certainly this second step had been taken in Antioch shortly after—in all likelihood even before—the second trip of Paul to Jerusalem. When the first steps were taken to disregard circumcision as a requirement for membership is impossible to say, but again it is highly probable that such disregard was being at least tolerated at a comparatively early date. Even in orthodox Judaism a missionary, as in the case of Izates, might hesitate to lay upon his converts this onerous demand.[26] The fact that it was a real obstacle to the reception of many male Gentiles attracted by the message of the early preachers may well have led to its quiet disregard. Certainly, quite regardless of whether Titus was or was not circumcised—the ambiguous phrasing of Gal. 2:3 ff. by no means lessens our dilemma—the mere mention of this situation indicates that already the problem had arisen.

How far Paul had gone along these lines of thought during these years in and around Antioch is hard to say. Some things would seem certain: Paul had come to be a figure of dominating importance in the Antioch church; by the time he went to Jerusalem, with Barnabas and Titus, he had definitely come to the conviction that his sphere of activity was the Gentile world. Thus, two conclusions would seem unquestionable. That during these years—so tantalizingly undescribed in any detail by Paul—he had already begun what later was to be his practice, a continuous mission of travel in the Gentile world, is uncertain and perhaps unlikely. That this style of mission was soon to be adopted by him, perhaps as a definite consequence of his visit to Jerusalem and sparked by the rift in Antioch shortly afterward, seems to me very likely. That during these years he established churches in "Syria and Cilicia" is possible but cannot be proved. The absence of any letters to them means nothing. The only reason we have letters during his later years of travel is that problems had arisen in some of these churches while he was far distant from them. Unable to go in person, he wrote a letter. During these years in "Syria and Cilicia," in all likelihood with a large, if not a major part of the time spent in Antioch, that need for writing was not acute, for, if necessary, a quick visit would always have been possible.

Most important of all: during these years Paul had come to the conclusion that Gentiles, not Jews, were to be his one concern, and that this had been God's intention. The momentous decision appears to have had a very simple start. His change of front from opponent to champion of the crucified but triumphant Jesus had not been due to any dissatisfaction with Jewish belief or practice. And his first endeavors had been among his fellow Jews, with the initial confidence of immediate success. This had not been realized. The obstacle of the cross—

and that meant the Law, which had so ominously decreed—proved stubborn and not to be gainsaid. For other preachers, apparently for some of those in Jerusalem, it was possible to escape the dilemma. For one like Paul, no avoidance of the main issue was possible. With no coolness to the Law to lead him to another solution, this man who moved on springs found the answer in the unexpected opposition which he received from Israel and the acceptance of his words by Gentiles. Whatever held his fellows blind to the light and deaf to the call of God must be a hindrance and something to be attacked. It was clearly the Law that taught what God had so clearly demonstrated was in error. Gentiles, unhampered by that dread fear, were more ready to hear and accept.

By the shattering experience which Paul had had, of seeing the risen and triumphant Jesus, which not only had convinced him of the folly of his opposition, but had also convinced him that this triumphant Jesus was God's superlative gift to men and the way to proper union and right relation with him, another door was opened. The one and only act of consequence was humbly and gratefully to accept God's gift. The story of Abraham stood crystal-clear. It was not Abraham's painful keeping in every detail an all-inclusive law that made God's favor the proper and deserved pay for Abraham's obedience. It was not by circumcision that Abraham had found the way to God's favor open. Instead, Abraham "believed in God," with all that meant, and God "reckoned it to him for righteousness" (Gal. 3:6; Gen. 15:6).

Many of the details in this line of thinking were to be worked out and developed in consequence of problems and difficulties encountered in his ministry. The basis of what was to be his gospel was the confidence that flashed upon him in the all-including vision of the triumphant Lord, the confidence that access to God and his favor came as God's unmerited gift to man, not as a reward or wage for man's obedience or service. But all this happened to Abraham quite apart from his circumcision. Thus, whatever values circumcision might have—

and Paul, as we have seen, proudly insists that some such values were his—it in no sense is the avenue or *sine qua non* to
God's freely offered grace. Furthermore—and Paul is always
the very practical and down-to-earth realist despite his often
labored and even awkward thinking—the demand for circumcision would close many opening doors. It would be as absurd
to block Gentiles from accepting God's Son—the embodiment
of his wisdom and love—by demanding circumcision, as to
deny fellowship to Jews because they did not flock to Jerusalem three times a year from wherever they might chance to be
residing.

Thus to take God's revelation and to make it simply a law-
book forbidding this and demanding that, with the understanding that one hundred percent compliance would result in
an adequate bank balance, was more than folly. Man's acts
were at best inconsequential (Paul was an Oriental, not a
Greek); it was God's action that counted: grace, not law, was
the one imperative. In a word, Paul's growing opposition to
the Law was due to the fact that the Law patently neglected
God's so manifestly all-important revelation in Jesus, whom he
had sent for a purpose and had uniquely exalted. The Law not
only neglected this but stood opposed to it. It pronounced as a
verdict of God what was clearly false, for God's act in raising
Jesus disproved it. It prevented men from hearkening to, and
obeying, God's ringing call. It led to their unwarranted and arrogant confidence that by their attendance to sundry demands
—many of which were impossible for them to meet—they
would receive as their due the expected reward. This blinded
their eyes to the patent fact that God was no paymaster of
earned wages—"Reward me for the noble way I have kept
your demands!"—but the Sovereign who not only freely bestowed his undeserved gift but himself provided men with the
insight to see and accept.

The Law was "holy, and the commandment holy and righteous and good" (Rom. 7:12). Never, regardless of how his
thought might develop, did Paul find himself opposed to the

Law. It had set his outlook on life from his earliest days, and he regularly not only cited its authority but appealed to it in support of his many demands. Actually, Christ was the fulfillment of the Law, when the latter was seen in its proper nature as God's revelation of himself. Paul found himself in —man's fatal mistake in seeking to justify himself by his meticulous, blind, and at times so-unsuccessful efforts.

7 | ANTIOCH AND JERUSALEM

"... for me also unto the Gentiles"

Following what would seem to be a chronological order of events during these early years after his conversion, Paul remarks:

> Then after the space of fourteen years [which space I have suggested may well be shortened to "four years," i.e., ca. A.D. 46/47] I went up again to Jerusalem with Barnabas, taking Titus also with me. (Gal. 2:1.)

Although Paul does not specifically mention the place from which this second visit to Jerusalem originated, it would seem highly probable that it originated from Antioch. This assumption in nowise depends upon the account in Acts, which latter would seem to be Luke's own deduction or reconstruction based on Paul's laconic statements.[27] Rather, it is a highly likely hypothesis based on Paul's own statements: (1) the period of time in "Syria and Cilicia"; and (2) the high probability, as certainly suggested by Gal. 2:11-21, that during this time Paul had become a prominent figure in the church at Antioch. Certainly the way this section is recounted implies that it was a close sequel to the statement about the visit in Jerusalem, which immediately precedes it. This is to me the chief weakness in the not unattractive thesis occasionally made, notably by Donald Riddle[28] and John Knox,[29] that the visit was from Ephesus and corresponds to the trip indicated in Acts 18:18-21. This suggestion has the merit of seeming to explain Paul's concern, when subsequently revisiting the churches which he had founded during these intervening years,[30] for the collection of the gift for the Jerusalem church. The weak links in the otherwise seemingly solid chain are a dependence on Acts for this Ephesus-Jerusalem (?) visit and a conspicuous failure to account for the incident in Antioch (Gal. 2:11-21). Why on their theory Paul lingered in Antioch (seemingly, at least, a dominant figure in this group) instead of continuing the course of action which for so many years had become his way of life, they do not seem to consider. Thus I would hazard the guess that Paul had spent this period of time in and around Antioch and that as yet his career as an itinerant to far distant centers had not begun, although more and more he had devoted himself to preaching to Gentiles.

With regard to the question, What led him to make this second visit to Jerusalem?—if we limit ourselves to Paul's own statements, disregarding Luke's seemingly so plausible explanations, we, like Luke, must be satisfied to guess. One thing seems clear: Paul did not go—nor was he sent by others —in obedience to a demand from the authorities in Jerusalem. Paul's whole argument hinges on that point; he stresses his complete independence from those who were "apostles before me." He is recounting these facts in answer to charges which had been brought against him in Galatia, charges which to him were cruel and perverse denial of his one basic confidence, namely, that his gospel had come to him direct from God's revelation, not from men's instruction. Thus his detailed and labored statements were to refute his critics, perhaps (as many believe) in the form: "I have not proved false, as you wickedly insist, to what I learned from the more authoritative apostles, for I never learned anything at all from them." Perhaps, as seems to me more likely, his statements were directed to Gentile critics in his Galatian churches who had easily accepted his gospel of freedom from the Law. These critics had gagged at what they thought to be his Judaizing demands. They were charging him, despite his brave words to the contrary, with camouflaging the fact that he was a Jew at heart and was seeking to load them with precisely the obligations from which he had claimed they and he were alike free.[31]

Thus his word, "And I went up by revelation," is certainly to be understood as the clearest sort of denial that he had gone up to Jerusalem through any sort of compulsion, either from Jerusalem or from colleagues in Antioch who thought such a gesture would be a wise conciliation. The words "by revelation" in the mouth of Paul are crystal-clear. To the prophet, what he says and does is not due to any one or any thing save God. Realistically interpreted, this means: the prophet himself is the source of his action. He "knows" he is right, and that is the end of it; he does not hearken to, nor is he influenced by, the advice or compulsion of others. In short, "I went up by revelation" means, "I went up because I had determined that that was what I was to do," or, more briefly stated, "I went up because I wanted to."

The "why" of Paul's determination to go up to Jerusalem— this also seems explainable. The repeated mention of the conviction that his was, and was to be, a ministry to the Gentiles is very significant (cf. Gal. 2:2, 3, 7-9). Obviously, by this time Paul had so concluded. Any earlier dreams of simply aiding his fellow Jews to bypass the dread obstacle of the cross, which had so troubled him, was long past. To think that this meant that he would refuse all contact with Jews and deny them admission to the gospel call is nonsense. Whosoever will may come! But he now was convinced that his field of labor was the Gentile world; and, of course, to the prophet that meant that such was and always had been God's purpose and plan for him. Furthermore, that he had already found himself successful in this activity could hardly fail to convince him that his choice of service was God-inspired.

Can we go farther? Had he reached the decision to cut free

from Antioch and other nearby cities? We know him from repeated statements in his letters as a man unwilling to labor in
another's field or to linger in fields already reaped. Was he de-
termining to move abroad, to seek uncultivated fields? Was it
this decision which led him to desire, before he started for
these fruitful fields, to avoid all unnecessary difficulties which
might hamper his work? Despite the fact that Paul was a vi-
sionary (at least he could see visions!), despite the fact that
he might believe the world was soon to end in a very near "to-
morrow," he was a man of amazing common sense, with feet
solidly planted on this earth. Years later, when his plans and
dreams were being centered on a trip to far-off Spain, which
he hoped to reach on an extended tour via Rome, he made
very careful plans to avoid unnecessary trouble in Rome,
where he well knew he might easily incur suspicion. To avoid
this he wrote them a letter, carefully indicating his plan. He
definitely did not plan to take over control in their church,
whatever rumors might have reached them to the contrary.
Furthermore, he was not as black as he was painted by his
enemies, and this *confessio fidei* might well disabuse them of
these prejudices. All this reveals very clearly the sort of man
Paul was, never wont to stumble if an ounce of common sense
would prevent it.

Thus I am inclined to wonder if a not dissimilar situation
was now before his mind. He might well be unknown by face
to many in Jerusalem, which was in sober fact the mother
church of the movement; it is certainly unlikely that reports of
his work among Gentiles, whom he was welcoming in increasing numbers, and without the benefit of circumcision or other
ceremonial restrictions, had failed to reach this Judean center.
It would be very wise to have a brief session with those who
conceivably might seriously interfere with the success of his
plans, and to convince them that they had nothing to fear in
his God-directed and God-blessed mission. His mission was
not of his own choice. None less than God had called him. His
credentials were surely as valid as any of theirs. Christ had ap-

peared to him as he had to Cephas (Peter), to James, and to
others of the apostles. More than that, this revelation had been
the last of these definitive epiphanies—the climax and culmination of the empowering of those destined to spread the
word (I Cor. 15:3-11). Surely those in Jerusalem, as well as
Paul himself, had but one object: to make disciples everywhere so that when the Lord returned, as he speedily would,
he should find faith in the earth. Thus it appears to me highly
probable that the trip to the south was the conscious prelude
to the next chapter of his mission, and that its purpose was to
avoid any impediments or obstacles which unfounded suspicion or misinformation might prompt.

And apparently this commonsense precaution proved, at
least in part, successful. Despite some opposition, certainly
hinted at in the reference to the "false brethren privily
brought in" (Gal. 2:4), who sought to make his visit his
downfall, Paul convinced the leaders that his plan to go to the
Gentiles was of a sort to which they could agree. Seemingly
Barnabas, who had accompanied Paul to Jerusalem, was to be
his comrade on the new quest. Later events were to make this
impossible, but at the moment, while in Jerusalem, they stood
shoulder to shoulder. As Paul tersely but clearly epitomizes
the visit, there is no hint of any attempt by the Jerusalem leaders, despite the desire of some "false brethren"—not Jews (as
Luke later was to insist), but Jewish Christians—to demand
that Paul conform to their practice, demand circumcision, and
refuse table fellowship with all who were not so made ready.
That this decision to recognize and at least not to oppose
Paul's purposed mission was enthusiastic, Paul has not said.
My impression, as I read the brief statement, is that it was not,
but that whatever the reluctance of some might have been, it
seemed wise to the leaders to recognize what they could not
easily prevent. Paul's reference to their perceiving "the grace
that was given unto me" (Gal. 2:9) is seemingly double-
barreled: his claim to having had a God-given vision of the triumphant Christ, if believed, was not to be minimized; his
marked success in making converts could not be denied.

Paul's concluding word to the mention of this episode is of especial interest:

> Provided only that we should remember the poor; which was the very thing I too was most ready to do. (Gal. 2:10.)

The general purport of these words is clear: this was the sole requirement demanded by the Jerusalem leaders in connection with their agreement, and Paul was more than willing to accept this obligation. However, many smaller points are uncertain. The absence of any main verb, usually understood by the English translators in their inserted "they would," implies that the clause was no additional request but a part of the agreement reached. Two questions arise. (1) Is the present subjunctive of the verb, "we should remember," futuristic ("this is what we were to do") or continuative ("this is what we had been doing and were to continue")? (2) Similarly, how significant is the change from the first person plural, "we should remember," to the first person singular, "I too was most ready to do"? Regarding (1), I feel there is a slightly greater probability for the meaning "this was to be our promised obligation." It is of course possible that Paul and his comrades had brought with them a tactful gift.[32] My guess is that this was the understanding of Luke as he read these words and that this led to his mention of the famine and the relief sent by Antioch. Regarding (2), it would seem that the plural is the natural reflection of the Jerusalem leaders' understanding of the now divided responsibility: you folks and we. The first singular is strictly accurate. When Paul wrote these words about the remembered compact, he and Barnabas had long since parted ways. As for the Galatians, when Paul was writing, he (Paul) was the only member with whom they were concerned.

Why the Jerusalem leaders had seen fit to stipulate this assistance is far from clear. Earlier stories in Acts about the enthusiastic selling of property, pooling the realized sums, and living off capital (Acts 2:43-47; 4:32-5:11)—all apparently based on the passionate certainty that the end was at hand, and the disastrous famine which beset Palestine "in the days of Claudius" (Acts 11:27 ff.)—might seem to make the request natural, but there is nothing in Paul's own material to throw any light upon, or to authenticate Luke's suggestion.

On the other hand, it is very natural to see the references to the collection which Paul has engineered from his Gentile churches and which he is planning to carry to Jerusalem prior to his departure for Rome and the West as the fulfillment of this accepted obligation. And many have been the efforts by commentators and other scholars so to conclude. The principal objection to this assumed connection is the length of time which would seem to have elapsed between the time of the promise and the time of its fulfillment.

I am inclined to view the matter a bit differently. To me it seems very possible that the reason for the Jerusalem leaders so to have qualified their endorsement was their insistence that this proposed division of the field—they to the circumcision, Paul and his fellows to the Gentiles—should not result in two mutually exclusive churches. Hence they would insist that such Gentile churches as might be established should be keenly aware of their fellowship with, and common obligation to, the original churches. Nor should it be forgotten that Paul is making reference to this decision and argument several years later and at the time when he is planning to push further west. In these new plans and dreams he has every desire, as we have seen, to let nothing interfere. A generous gift from these Gentile churches to the mother church in Jerusalem might well be a convincing proof that the body of Christ was in no way dismembered by the Gentile mission ("all one body we"). Thus I am inclined to see Paul's so obvious concern that the gift be raised, and that it be a worthy one, very prominent in his thought during the closing months of his service in the East, during which the letters mentioning the gift were written. This may account for the fact that in the letter to the Galatians—written in precisely this period of concern—Paul may have allowed his phrasing of the earlier event to have been influenced by his present concern, giving later readers the unwarranted confidence that what he was later to do was in exact and literal compliance with the request earlier laid upon him. If this possibility be allowed, it would seem at best uncertain, if not actually unlikely, that the insistence of Jerusalem upon unbroken fellowship took the form of a demand for financial assistance—regular, intermittent, or in the form of a sizable gift at some subsequent period.

Paul passionately attacked the contention of his opponents that his claim to independence from the oversight and control of Jerusalem in the early years of his mission was grossly unwarranted. This led to his recounting various incidents in these years which provide us with seemingly accurate coordinates for sketching a curve of his career. To those already considered, the next paragraph in Galatians is an important addition: the vivid picture of events in Antioch incident to successive visits there by Peter (Cephas) and "certain from James." Certainly as one reads Galatians, there is nothing to suggest that the sequence of incidents is artificial. The introductory words, "But when Cephas came to Antioch," seem to be the introduction to an event subsequent to the one just mentioned. Occasionally this has been challenged and the visit of Peter to Antioch placed prior to Paul's visit to Jerusalem. There is nothing in the language of the passages to support this assumption, which certainly does violence to what may be styled the "psychological probabilities of the situation." That any such reconstruction would ever have been attempted save as a consequence of trying to force Paul's own words in his letters into the artificial framework of Acts is more than doubtful. Freed from this unnecessary burden, we are freed from the necessity of devising explanations more taxing to credulity than the problems they seek to explain.

Sometime after the return of Paul and his companions to Antioch Peter seems to have arrived. The reason for his visit is

not explained. That it was in any sense supervisory, as Acts so
regularly suggests was the habit of the apostles, is unlikely. As
would appear not improbable, it was like those which Acts has
suggested that Peter had made to Joppa and Caesarea. Since
in the next verse mention is made of a delegation from Jerusalem—"certain from James"—it is tempting to wonder if
we do not have hints here of the reason for the transfer from
Peter to James of leadership in the Jerusalem church and for
the disappearance of Peter. As the number of disciples in-
creased and opposition to them heightened, it is highly probable that the Jerusalem church became increasingly careful to
avoid suspicion of being un-Jewish or indifferent to ancestral
practices. In consequence, those inclined to be less exacting
toward compliance found farther fields fairer.

In Antioch apparently the second step had already been
taken: not only were Gentiles welcomed without a demand
that they be circumcised, but they were granted free table fellowship. Seemingly the latter practice had not been discussed
by Paul and the Jerusalem leaders during his visit. There, in
Jerusalem, "freedom from the Law" had been limited to waiv-
ing the requirement that Gentiles be circumcised. Here in Antioch is to be found the second step: here "freedom from the
Law" meant that Jews might eat with uncircumcised Gentiles.
And Peter apparently seemed to acquiesce. When, however,
others from Jerusalem arrived, who were far from placid at
this violation, Peter became self-conscious and sought to ease
himself out of this embarrassing predicament. This is enough
to make clear that this violation of the proprieties of the Jewish food laws was apparently the practice in Antioch and no
innovation suggested by Peter; it also suggests that it had not
been his own practice. Rather, when in Rome it is all right to
do as the Romans do, so long as there are none present from
the home town to see you.

Seemingly the protests of those "from James," supported by
Peter's embarrassed withdrawal, led other Jews, including
Barnabas, to follow. As a result the harmony and fellowship of

the Antiochian church, which had apparently charmed Peter on his first arrival and had led him to join in without thinking the problem through, was disrupted, and Paul bitterly protested, rebuking Peter publicly. To what extent the rest of the chapter is a literal transcript of Paul's protest to Peter is uncertain. There is enough evidence that the clash was far from a momentary flash in the pan. Again, if we did not have the later account in Acts to blind our eyes, we would definitely incline to feel that as a result of this dispute the ways of Paul and his erstwhile colleague definitely parted, for in none of his letters does Paul refer to Barnabas as a companion on his journeys.

The author of Acts, with his constant effort to minimize contentions of any sort among Christians and to limit all hostility to the acts of Jews, not only entirely omits this scene in Antioch but seemingly attempts to explain away the contention between Paul and Barnabas by the story of their separation because of Mark's withdrawal at Pisidian *Antioch* (Acts 15: 36-39; cf. ch. 13:13).

To what extent the breach in the Antioch church was healed is not indicated. Seemingly Paul had come to have a position of prominence, if not of actual leadership, in the church. Did this collision alter this relation? We can only guess. It is to my mind highly probable that it acted as the final spur to set Paul on his course as a traveling missionary. It is quite possible that he was already considering some such step when he made his visit to Jerusalem. Apparently, even if he was, he had not instantly started but had returned to Antioch. It is likely that there had been an appreciable lapse of time—perhaps some months—between this visit and the arrival of Peter in Antioch. To me it is very probable that the action of the Jewish Christians in Antioch in yielding to the protests from Jerusalem alienated Paul or at least catalyzed his plans for a new and altogether-other sort of ministry, and that shortly after this episode he severed his contact with the Antiochian church. Once again the author of Acts seeks to minimize all traces of dissension. He can use, but cannot afford to quote, the Pauline letters, for they are far too full of what to Luke was definitely not for publication. He can picture the Antiochian Christians in all peace and harmony fasting, praying, and laying their hands on "Barnabas and Saul" (Acts 13:1-3), and thus being responsible for the real Gentile mission Paul was to accomplish. And once again the picture arising from fragments in the Pauline letters appears far more convincing, although shorn of many details, than the account from the facile pen of his biographer and creator.

8 | THE GENTILE MISSION

Light from the letters

With the episode in Antioch—with Paul's attack on Peter; the loss of Barnabas; and the apparent falling away from a proper understanding of the gospel, as it seemed to Paul, of a sizable part of the Antiochians—our convenient chronological sequence of events in Paul's early years as a Christian protagonist ends. That he left Antioch shortly after this time of disillusionment is highly probable. The fortunate preservation of several of his letters provides us (as it seemingly provided Luke) with material from which we can have a picture, at times even a detailed one, both of the gospel Paul preached and of the folk and places in which he preached it.

We have letters to Galatia, Philippi, Thessalonica, and Corinth. It is certainly highly probable that these indicate regions Paul visited and in that consecutive order. A glance at the map will surely justify that assumption. It is not to be overlooked that Paul seemingly found himself at home in cities. His earlier stay in Damascus and Antioch hint in that direction; the fact that in his later career a series of important cities —Philippi, Thessalonica, Athens, Corinth, Ephesus—became centers[33] for his work makes the assumption warranted. These would be of the greatest strategic value in his God-given necessity of sounding forth God's imperative call. As we look at the districts suggested by the letters, Galatia may at first seem a contradiction. That those he addresses as "foolish Galatians" are to be seen as residents of what was the old kingdom of Galatia, centering about Ancyra, and not Phrygians and Lycaonians living in such cities as Pisidian Antioch, Iconium, Lystra, and Derbe, is highly probable and certainly would never have been doubted had not Acts chronicled visits to these latter with no mention of the former. But what led Paul to this strategically unlikely rural region? The answer to this query is seemingly provided by a word in the letter:

> But ye know that because of an infirmity of the flesh I preached the gospel unto you the first time: and that which was a temptation to you in my flesh ye despised not, nor rejected. (Gal. 4:13-14.)

Apparently he had not gone to Galatia for that purpose, but had fallen sick while passing through, and thus had utilized this unexpected circumstance to sound forth his word. It appears highly probable that he had been en route to Ephesus but had been prevented from entering the province of Asia and had accordingly been forced to modify his plan and to turn north.

Quite regardless of these details, the letter itself indicates that Paul had visited this district, not improbably twice.[34] It is certainly likely that this district may plausibly be regarded as the first of those to whom letters were subsequently written, for, of them all, this was the nearest to Antioch. Philippi would apparently be the next port of call after his recovery and departure from Galatia. From Philippi he went to Thessalonica. This is not only a likely assumption as we consider the geographical location of the various places which his letters prove he visited, but is indicated clearly by his word to the Thessalonians: "But having suffered before and been shamefully treated, as ye know, at Philippi, we waxed bold in our God to speak unto you the gospel of God in much conflict" (I Thess. 2:2). From Thessalonica he had proceeded south to Athens (I Thess. 3:1). The absence from our *corpus Pauli-*

narum of a letter to Athens strongly suggests that his visit to that city did not result in the establishment of a church for which he felt a lasting responsibility, as in the cases of Galatia, Philippi, and Thessalonica. From Athens he apparently proceeded to Corinth, another strategic center, as had been Philippi and Thessalonica. In Corinth, as his several letters to that city clearly show, he had spent considerable time, and he subsequently revisited it at least twice.

Thus there were four European centers—Philippi, Thessalonica, Athens, and Corinth—which we know from his letters he visited and labored in. There seems little ground for questioning that he reached them in this order. That his stay in each of them, with the possible exception of Athens, was of considerable duration is certainly highly probable. The later account, dividing his ministry into several consecutive journeys, with constant returns to Antioch, is certainly not demanded by the letters themselves, and can be—and has been—very misleading. For example, the seeming limitation of his stay in Thessalonica to two or three weeks[35] is improbable in view of Paul's own word to the Thessalonians about having worked—presumably at his trade—"night and day" (I Thess. 2:9) so as not to be a burden to them, and of his grateful mention to his friends in Philippi of the aid they had sent him "once and again" (Phil. 4:16) while he was in Thessalonica. Freed from the necessity of viewing these periods of activity as hasty visits, we get much more probable—though usually, unfortunately, not detailed—pictures of a period of years of progressive activity in these areas in western Asia and eastern Europe. And a word such as that in Rom. 15:19 ("so that from Jerusalem, and round about even unto Illyricum, I have fully preached the gospel of Christ") certainly suggests that during his periods of lengthy stay in these several strategic centers he had not remained all the time in the city itself but had made long trips into the surrounding areas, either himself or through lieutenants whom he sent. For example, Epaphras went to Colossae and Laodicea during Paul's sojourn in Ephesus.

Thus it appears probable that between the time when he left Antioch and the time of his departure from Corinth after his first visit there was a period of several years. During these years the only letter which has come down to us is I Thessalonians, which was apparently written from Corinth, shortly after Paul's arrival there from Athens. If II Thessalonians is to be regarded as coming from the pen of Paul, it too would come from that same center and but shortly after the first letter. In my judgment it is wiser to see this letter (which is so mechanically a replica of I Thessalonians, save for its central section, ch. 2:1-12, and that seems definitely un-Pauline) as a post-Pauline writing by a later disciple striving to answer a new challenge as he believed his dead master would have done, and striving to make his letter seem Pauline by slavishly copying, as Paul himself would scarcely have done.

With this exception, the bulk of our extant letters appears to have been written from Ephesus during the long period in which this important center had apparently been Paul's headquarters. How Paul had reached Ephesus is uncertain. There is nothing in any of our letters to throw any direct light on this subject. According to the account in Acts, Paul had left Corinth following his fruitless arrest and arraignment before the Roman governor, Gallio, due to the malice of the Corinthian Jews. After a short visit to Ephesus and a promise speedily to return, he had sailed to Caesarea, en route to Antioch. Then from Antioch he had gone overland, via Galatia, this time successfully reaching Ephesus. But of this trip to Antioch (and conceivably Jerusalem) there is no hint in any of the letters; hence it is wisely omitted in our attempt to limit our source of information to those materials of which we can be sure.

During his stay in Ephesus, which was presumably spent in establishing new churches both in the city itself and throughout the area (cf. his word to the Corinthians, "the churches of Asia salute you"—I Cor. 16:19), Paul kept in touch with the churches which he had earlier organized and for which he continued to have concern. It may well be that during this period, in addition to writing to them, he made return trips to some of these earlier churches. We can be certain that he made a second trip to Corinth from Ephesus: difficulties which had arisen in the isthmus city caused him such alarm that in addition to two corrective letters he had made a hasty trip back across the Aegean. In addition, it would appear to me not improbable that during this same period he had gone east to Galatia to straighten out a difficulty of which word had reached him, and, not impossibly, also to insist on their participation in the collection he was now planning to take to Jerusalem. In both cases—Corinth and Galatia—these hasty visits had proved highly unsuccessful and had led the disturbed apostle, upon his forced return to Ephesus, from which apparently he felt it unwise to be absent too long, to pen very severe letters—II Cor., chs. 10 to 13, and Galatians.

We have no detailed picture of his stay in Ephesus, but occasional words indicate that it had been a trying and taxing time: "for a great door and effectual is opened unto me, and there are many adversaries" (I Cor. 16:9). His mention of one difficulty ("If after the manner of men I fought with beasts at Ephesus"—I Cor. 15:32) is probably not to be understood as an experience in the arena, from which even Paul, despite his later romancers, would likely not have escaped alive, but it does indicate a time of storm and stress. Nor is the ominous word early in the letter we style II Corinthians to be overlooked:

> For we would not have you ignorant, brethren, concerning our difficulties which befell us in Asia, that we were weighed down exceedingly, beyond our power, insomuch that we despaired even of life: yea, we ourselves have had the sentence of death within ourselves, that we should not trust in ourselves, but in God who raiseth the dead: who delivered us out of so great a death . . .[36]

Undoubtedly his distress and uncertainty about the fates of his churches in Corinth and Galatia,[37] to whom he had recently paid fruitless visits and subsequently had written extravagant letters of reproach which he had regretted as soon as they had been sent, were a real factor in his gloom at departing from Ephesus to Macedonia; but in Ephesus itself he had faced more than successful hostility.

In all likelihood, no small part of that stay had been in prison. That the letters to Philippi, Colossae, and Philemon, obviously all three written from prison, stem from Ephesus is highly probable and is coming so to be regarded by an increasing number of investigators.[38] Certainly the amount of travel indicated in the letter to Philippi—they had heard of his imprisonment and had sent Epaphroditus (Phil. 4:18) to aid him; Epaphroditus had fallen sick, and news of that mishap had got back to Philippi; Paul had heard of the Philippians' resultant concern (Phil. 2:25 ff.)—makes the comparatively nearby Ephesus far less unlikely than such distant places as Caesarea or Rome, in both of which, according to Acts, Paul had been imprisoned. Similarly, the likelihood is real that it was to Ephesus—not distant Rome or Caesarea—that Onesimus had fled from his master, Philemon. In addition, there was Paul's expectation of speedily coming to Philippi (Phil. 2:24; cf. also ch. 1:27) and his casual remark to Philemon:

> But withal prepare me also a lodging: for I hope that through your prayers I shall be granted unto you. (Philemon 22.)

All these combine to make Ephesus the most likely spot for this prison correspondence. If this be the case, confident classification of the several letters as "early" and "late" needs definite reconsideration. Incidentally (at the moment the proponents of this view are very vocal), the confident discovery of constant and steady development in Paul's methodically expanding theological thought processes, enabling the critics (but rarely in unison) to dissect and rearrange the resulting sections of the several letters in a sort of upward-and-onward spiral, appears to me far from impressive.

Finally Paul left Ephesus—he had planned to leave shortly after Pentecost (I Cor. 16:8), but seemingly had been forced to remain longer. He had earlier planned to make an overland trek through Macedonia (Philippi and Thessalonica) to Corinth. As he left Ephesus in the deepest of depression, he had apparently given up his earlier plan to go to Corinth. Affairs there had blazed out of control. His hasty trip had but added to the already mounting flames; his bitter letter, seemingly penned as soon as he returned to Ephesus, and no sooner sent than regretted, had led him to feel that a subsequent visit would be worse than useless. If, as seems to me quite possible, his return to Ephesus from Corinth had been greeted with an equally depressing word about matters in Galatia, this could well account for the marked similarity in tone, but not, of course, in content, between the two extravagant letters, II Cor., chs. 10 to 13 (commonly styled "the severe letter") and Galatians (equally aptly described as "blotted with tears of anger," and replete with exaggerations he was later to regret). They were written at the same time by the nervously distraught and harried man: Corinth ablaze, Galatia torn with dissension, Ephesus—the city, if not the church—bitterly hostile. Small wonder that under these circumstances, in these letters, Paul is to be seen as qualifying for the descriptive phrase "God's angry man."

Apparently Titus, who had carried this "severe letter" to Corinth, had succeeded in staying the storm. At any rate, he meets Paul somewhere in Macedonia with the amazingly good news that the opposition in Corinth had broken down. The leader of the rebellion had been discountenanced and the church was eager for Paul's return. In relief and joy—his emotions could swing him like a pendulum—Paul wrote the letter we now know as II Cor., chs. 1 to 9, or at least a substantial part of it. In addition to a distinctly moving, if somewhat ponderous and labored, explanation of why he had written so severe a reproof (with its undertone, familiar to most fathers, "I did it because I loved you; it hurt me more than it did you")

he reverted to the matter of the sizable collection he was taking in his Gentile churches for the Jerusalem church. As I
have already remarked, this collection may in some degree be
connected with the expectation expressed by the Jerusalem
leaders years before at the time of Paul's visit. Be that as it
may, Paul's thinking was now turned to the West—his work in
the East was nearly at an end. For Paul, the decision to visit
Jerusalem and to prove that his work had not been divisive
but of the sort to cement all Christians the closer together had
come to seem increasingly wise. It appears to me not at all impossible that this insistence that his churches make that contribution had been, at least in part, significant in the disruption
both in Corinth and Galatia. In the same breath (as it might
well have seemed to many of his Gentile hearers) he had
insisted that they were free from Jewish constraints and
controls, as was he. He had pretended not to wish their financial assistance but had made a to-do about always working
with his own hands. Now he was putting the heat on to raise a
large amount of money, which he claimed was to go to those
from whom he had broken free. Such may well have been the
attitude of many. It is not difficult to imagine the wrath of
some of the Galatians who were thus simply reinforced in
their confidence that despite his brave words Paul was, and always had been, simply a yes-man for the crowd in Jerusalem.

The rebellion in Corinth had now been stayed—apparently
Titus had proved strong where Timothy had so signally failed
that even Paul's impetuous quick visit had proved fruitless.
Therefore not only did Paul gladly determine to visit the isthmus city again, to collect their love gift, and to carry it by sea
to Jerusalem, but he so advised the church there by another
letter (II Cor., chs. 1 to 9), which he sent by Titus. Mean-
while he himself revisited, for what he believed would be the
last time, his churches in Macedonia.

After some months in the north he proceeded to Corinth,
apparently expecting that his stay in that city would mark the
end of his mission in the Near East (Asia Minor and Greece).

During his stay in Corinth, together with completing his plan for the return to Jerusalem prior to departing for the as yet untouched West, he wrote another letter, in some respects the most significant of his whole correspondence and apparently the last letter to come from his pen: Romans.

That this letter was at first intended for Rome is most unlikely. There are many indications of this, all of which have been constantly discussed and need not be debated again: the absence of any mention of Rome in Rom. 1:7, 15, in several manuscripts; the utter inappropriateness of Rom., ch. 16, in a letter to Rome; the comment of Origen that Marcion had cut away everything after ch. 14:23; the failure of many Fathers to quote any section of chs. 15 and 16; and the list of chapter headings ("capitulations") found in many Vulgate manuscripts, which evidence a text limited to chs. 1:1 to 14:23 and ch. 16:25-27.[39]

Mention has already been made of the heated, often extravagant and overexaggerated, argument in Galatians. In that letter, which so clearly evidences the mental stress under which Paul was laboring, he had used every sort of argument to win his case, and again and again in anger had given expression to words which he subsequently regretted. Just as the tone of II Cor., chs. 10 to 13, and Galatians have much in common, so do the contents of Romans and Galatians. Again and again the same subjects are treated but with far more restraint in Romans. Thus it is tempting to wonder if there is not a real connection between the two similar, but also dissimilar, writings. To revert to the situation which seems so clear: greatly disturbed by the report which Timothy had brought back to Ephesus of the situation in Corinth, Paul had precipitately made a sudden and unexpected trip across the Aegean, although apparently he had been reluctant at the moment to leave Ephesus. Seemingly his visit had done more harm than good. He could not stay longer and left in a state of great unrest. Arriving back in Ephesus he had been greeted by a

most disturbing report from Galatia, a report which may or
may not have occasioned another and equally fruitless trip to
stay that unrest. The result was these blistering letters—the
one to Corinth, the other to the churches of Galatia.

Now, months later in Corinth, with these difficulties things
of the past, the memory of his heated and exaggerated words
to Galatia still worried him. He had explained to the Corinthians the reason for his heated words to them and the pain it
had caused him so to write; the actually un-Pauline statements
in Galatians still remained to rankle and disturb him. Thus I
am definitely inclined to see a desire of Paul to restate in coolness and balance what he had earlier dashed off in the excite-
ment of the moment (when he had penned his blistering
attack to the "foolish Galatians") as the real cause and
background of the letter we call Romans. Whether he actually
composed a second and cooler letter specifically to the Galatians, it is impossible to say. It may well be that in its composition, or in the thought that preceded the actual composition, a
possibility occurred to him: since what he was intending was
actually his *confessio fidei*, it might well be a most appropriate
bequest to all his churches among whom he had labored so
long and all of whom he loved so deeply.

That reflections in Romans are to be seen of many points
discussed in Paul's other letters—not alone the vexed matter of
the law and sin, so vibrant in Galatians, but other matters
such as the eating or not eating of meat conceivably offered to
idols, to choose but one example of many—is too conspicuous
an element in this letter we call "Romans" to demand more
than mere statement. It is useless to search this epistle for fancied evidence of the nature of the Roman church; it is more
than useful—it is imperative—to examine it for evidence of
the sort of man its author was. Not that it evidences, since it
was his last epistle, a little more growth than he shows in earlier writings ("every day, in every way, he was advancing
in theological development," is what so many today are
fancifully conceiving); on the contrary, it is the same Paul,

but he is at the moment more at ease. He is not chiding this church for this or reproving that church for that. Instead he is quietly and restrainedly seeking to set forth to all his churches his gospel as he had come to know and love it. Thus I like to style this letter "his last will and testament." That it was to be sent as a circular letter is possible, but far from certain. Rather, I would toy with the notion that he had several copies of it made and dispatched to his several churches whom he never again expected to see on this earth, and that this farewell *confessio fidei* consisted of chs. 1:1 to 14:23 (minus, of course, such local references to Rome as ch. 1:7, 15, and perhaps a few other minor variations) and ch. 15:1-13 and perhaps ch. 16:25-27, although I am far from certain that this so balanced and ornate conclusion was not produced and added when the letters were collected and edited, as a final benediction to the whole corpus. Not inconceivably, the several copies might have had occasional additions appropriate to the particular recipients. Thus it would appear to me likely that Rom., ch. 16, so conspicuously out of place in a letter intended for Rome and so obviously appropriate to Ephesus, whither Phoebe was removing, was a final and added chapter in the copy intended for Ephesus.

During this literary achievement—it was scarcely a job to be dashed off hurriedly in a day or two!—it may well have occurred to Paul that it would be a most tactful gesture to send a slightly emended copy to Rome, the city he hoped to visit en route to Spain. It would indicate to them the sort of man he was and thus would correct any mistaken notions that those Christians might have received from rumors and malicious misstatements. It could easily also free the Romans from any unwarranted fears that this possessive man of whom they had heard had any intent of taking over control of their church. Then in the draft intended for Rome as a sort of preventive, or prophylactic, the local allusions (ch. 1:7, 15) were inserted, and instead of ch. 15:1-13 he added ch. 15:14-33 as the final paragraph and end of the letter.

With the composition of this letter, intended as a final greeting and admonition to the several churches where he had labored, our firsthand source of knowledge of Paul ends. He is in Corinth, from which city he had earlier hoped to depart for Rome and the West. When he had written to Corinth from Ephesus regarding the collection for Jerusalem, which was then looming large in his thoughts, he had seemingly half hoped that he would not be forced to go personally to Jerusalem:

> And when I arrive [sc. in Corinth], whomsoever ye shall approve, them will I send with letters to carry your bounty unto Jerusalem: and if it be meet for me to go also, they shall go with me. (I Cor. 16:3-4.)

In the concluding chapters of his last letter to Corinth (II Cor., chs. 8 and 9), which were written from Macedonia, and which many scholars are inclined to see as originally independent short notes, there is no indication of how Paul was contemplating the delivery of the offering. In Romans, written a few months later, he had made up his mind to deliver the gift in person. What had led to this revision of his travel plans he has not indicated. Was it that the gift had assumed such proportions that he wished to safeguard its arrival? Was it in answer to earlier expressed suspicion as to his own disinterest which had led him to assure his churches—notably the one in Corinth—that their own delegates would accompany those bearing the gift to ensure its safe arrival, and which had led him to feel a similar precaution well advised? Was it that he had come to feel that a personal visit in Jerusalem, prior to his departure for the West, would be wise; that thereby he could be sure that the Jerusalem authorities were quite clear that his work among Gentiles had in nowise jettisoned the unity of the church? Since he has not answered these queries, it is idle to guess. One thing is very clear. He regarded the trip East with some concern, even trepidation, not merely because it would delay by some months his start for the West but also because he was far from sure as to the welcome he would receive:

> Now I beseech you, brethren, by our Lord Jesus Christ, and by the love of the Spirit, that ye strive together with me in your prayers to God for me; that I may be delivered from them that are disobedient in Judaea, and that my ministration which I have for Jerusalem may be acceptable to the saints; that I may come unto you [sc. in Rome] in joy through the will of God, and together with you find rest. (Rom. 15:30-32.)

Nor were these fears unfounded. His earlier experiences, both during the two previous visits to Jerusalem and subsequently in Antioch, to which "certain from James" had come, had been such as to make the visit, even with a sizable gift, most unpredictable.

Paul has given us no hint as to the way in which this necessary but ominous visit was to be accomplished. Did he plan to go direct by ship via Caesarea or by a longer and more time-consuming overland trek? He has not told us, and we do not know. Since in all likelihood Paul had not already picked up the several gifts from Galatia (I Cor. 16:1), Macedonia (II Cor. 9:4; Rom. 15:26), and Achaia (Rom. 15:26)—it is scarcely likely that he was venturing to carry so considerable a sum with him, unless he had been still uncertain as to his itinerary after reaching Corinth—perhaps the overland route is the more probable. This would enable him to be joined en route by the several delegates with their churches' gifts. That among the several hints, to this church and that, of the generosity already displayed by other churches in getting their offering ready, there is no mention of any such action on the part of the churches in Asia, notably Ephesus, is, to say the least, surprising.

That Paul reached Jerusalem—either by sea or by land—and eventually Rome is quite possible, even probable, but we

have no indication of this, save as hoped for, in our principal
source of knowledge. For those content to use the account in
Acts, particularly for those parts of Paul's career where no
word from him is available, this added chapter is, of course,
certain, and any hesitance or even caution will likely be regarded as hypercriticism.[40] Nonetheless, sober criticism of the
several colorful chapters in Acts which seek to record the days
after the final departure from Corinth cannot fail to see the account so conspicuously couched in what may be safely called
"Lukan style" that extreme caution would certainly seem demanded. Luke has a strong tendency to introduce the miraculous in startling prominence as he recounts the experiences of
his heroes, and there is a marked similarity in the stories:
Simon Magus in Samaria and Elymas in Crete (Acts 8:9-24;
13:4-12); Peter's miraculous release from prison and Paul's
from the Philippi jail (Acts 12:1-19; 16:19-40); Peter and Ananias in Jerusalem (Acts 5:1-11); Paul and Elymas in Crete
(Acts 13:4-12); Paul and the viper on Rhodes (Acts 28:1-6);
Paul raising Eutychus from the dead (Acts 20:7-12); the miraculous cures from touching handkerchiefs or aprons which
had had contact with Paul's body (Acts 19:11-12); speaking
with tongues in Jerusalem, understood in terms of a stupen-
dous miracle of heavenly linguistics (Acts 2:1-13). In short, to
what extent Luke is following other traditions in his account
of the trip to Jerusalem, the stay there, the Odyssey-like sea
voyage to Rome; to what extent he is faced with the same dilemma as we in completing the story of his hero Paul, whose
letters presumably left Luke stranded in Corinth—all this is
hard to say.

One thing is very certain, and to me it appears highly
revealing: in the Lukan tale there is a definite and conspicuous silence as to the reception of the collection by the church
in Jerusalem. He mentions the assembly at Corinth of Paul's
agents from Macedonia and Asia (Acts 20:4-6), but with no
explanation of why they were going to Jerusalem. In his
speech to Felix, Paul is made to refer to his having come to

Jerusalem "to bring alms to my nation, and offerings" (Acts 24:17)—the sole reference to this matter which Luke permits. And the reason for this exception is obvious and definitely "Lukan": It is to heighten Paul's innocence in the eyes of the Roman governor. His coming to Jerusalem had not been to foment trouble as his enemies so often maintained. Thus Luke's silence in the earlier tale of what had happened in Jerusalem prior to the outbreak from which the Roman centurion had rescued Paul is definitely heightened rather than lessened by this indication that the incident of the gift in money was known but deliberately bypassed.

Only one conclusion seems at all possible: the contribution failed lamentably to accomplish what Paul had hoped for. The resulting opposition, which Paul had dreaded, was not from Jerusalem Jews but from Jerusalem Jewish *Christians*. All this was highly distasteful to Luke, whose continued thesis was that the opposition which was so constantly met was from hostile Jews; Christians, be they Jews or Gentiles, had always been in hearty accord and good fellowship. Thus he drastically rewrote—or composed—the account, carefully omitting this dynamite, stressing Paul's scrupulous avoidance of giving offense, even representing Paul sponsoring the Nazirite vow of the nameless four (Acts 21:20-26). While the Tübingen school definitely overstressed their basic contention of the unending clash epitomized in Peter and Paul in their Hegelian roles of thesis and antithesis, they were probably nearer the facts in seeing this clash than was Luke in his unending attempt to obscure and hide this early chapter which had been substantially closed before he wrote. It is very hard to avoid the suspicion that the story of Simon Magus attempting to purchase the supernatural ability possessed by the apostles is a rewritten story of the hostility met by Paul as he tried to buy his way into the Christian circle.

To revert to an earlier word: That Paul reached Jerusalem and eventually Rome is quite possible, even probable. The seeming size of the collection renders it highly improbable that it was not delivered; Paul's manifest conviction that before turning west he must revisit Jerusalem certainly makes likely that he let nothing interfere with that determination to deliver it in person; he had a fear of the "disobedient in Judaea" and was apprehensive that his visit and gift might not prove acceptable to the saints—all these facts would seem to ensure the likelihood that he reached Jerusalem. But with that bare confidence we must be satisfied. To attempt to extract from the story which Acts has contrived from these "givens" an account of the journey and of the years in and near Jerusalem would appear to me unwarranted and of a sort very seriously to distort the story through forcing Paul in this later section upon the Lukan bed of Procrustes, from which we have hitherto sought to keep him, unstretched and unmutilated.

To this reconstruction of the life and activity of Paul, based solely on his letters, which can be properly styled the one severely historical source of our knowledge of him, one further note should be added. During the time of his missionary activity—subsequent to his departure from Antioch and prior to his final departure from Corinth—he wrote several letters to churches which he had established and for which he continued to feel a responsibility for leadership and direction. In no sense were they intended to give information to subsequent generations. Still less were they intended to supplement or replace canonical Scripture. They were letters in which advice and correction were penned solely because distance and the impossibility or impracticability of personal visits prevented the instruction being given orally. In no sense were they manuals of Christian theology, although the latest of them, known today as Romans, as has been emphasized, may properly be regarded as resembling a précis of what Paul might well have called his gospel. Most of the others were letters written to churches he had established and in which he had labored and taught. Thus they were not tracts for unbelievers; instead they were intended to answer questions which had arisen, to correct abuses and uncertainties which had arisen subsequent to his departure. Failure to consider this as we read and seek to understand the letters is certain to lead to disaster. For the most part they do not emphasize points—often even important points—where harmony and lack of misunderstanding prevailed between church and absent teacher. Instead, they were attempts to correct abuses or to answer questions. Thus to attempt their analysis mechanically—e.g., to assume that a long and detailed section indicates a point of major importance, while a brief statement signifies a matter of less significance— is most misleading. Precisely the opposite was frequently the case. Often it was a matter that Paul had apparently not felt significant enough to warrant full discussion during his weeks or months with them, that had subsequently led to uncertainty. In a word, they were letters from an "I" to a "you," not epistles which contained edifying material intended for any reader into whose hands it might come. And they are restricted to groups for which he felt responsibility and from which he was absent.

This at once accounts for the absence of letters to several communities in which Paul worked: Damascus, Antioch, Cilicia (?), and Athens. There is no probability that he established a church in Damascus or was in any sense in a position of responsibility for its well-being. In Antioch, too, the church was already in existence prior to his residence in the city. While the episode there in which the break with Peter and Barnabas occurred would suggest his prominence, even leadership, in the congregation, it was not his church, and when he left Antioch, not impossibly, as we have seen, as a result of the clash, he left with no further feeling of responsibility. So far as "Cilicia" is concerned, we can only surmise. While he may have established churches in Cilicia, there is no evidence of it in his writings, and it may well be that he carried on that sort of mission—to remoter districts in which no earlier work had been done—subsequent to his departure from Antioch. While in Antioch, he may well have restricted his work to districts near enough to that center so that, had any occasion arisen, he could have visited them instead of attempting to solve the problem by letter.

From the chance reference in I Thessalonians we know that he visited Athens. Even without its specific mention we might well have assumed the high probability that en route south from Thessalonica he would have visited Athens before moving on to Corinth. The absence of a letter to Athens or of any mention of the city in any of his other letters would certainly suggest that he was not successful in establishing there a church for which he felt subsequent responsibility. Very obviously this was the opinion of Luke. On the basis of Paul's early words in I Corinthians (Corinth was reached directly after Athens!) disparaging the wisdom of the wise and insisting, "I, brethren, when I came unto you, came not with excellency of speech or of wisdom" (I Cor. 1:18 ff.; 2:1 ff.), Luke was led to think that Paul had, so to speak, flunked his philosophy exam in Athens and had determined never again to attempt that fruitless approach. It was years later when Paul wrote I Corinthians and it was scarcely likely that the memory of his lack of success in Athens still eclipsed all else in Paul's eyes. These things would seem not to have been considered by Luke. Even if he did consider them, they did not appear to him of any moment. Certainly the account in Acts of the episode in Athens is simply another piece evidencing brilliant imagination of what a Jew in such a setting might have said, and similar in tone to the speech Luke puts into Paul's mouth at Lystra (Acts 14:8-18). That either speech is an actual report of what Paul said is most unlikely. His reported word about an altar with the inscription "To an unknown God" is most improbable. Altars with no inscriptions were quite possible; nor is it unlikely that even an altar or other memorial might have been erected in a spot believed to be numinous by some awestruck worshiper not sure of the proper deity to be worshiped there and so with the legend "To unknown gods." But "To an unknown God" is far more easily seen in the

mouth of Marcion than of Paul. I should definitely regard the
whole setting in Athens a brilliant piece of imaginative writing, evoked by the absence of any letter or even reference to
Athens as a site of Paul's successful efforts.

At first blush, the absence of a letter to Ephesus is more surprising. That the letter in our canon bearing that designation
is from the pen of Paul—at least to Ephesus—is most unlikely.
Three passages are sufficient to make this contention unan-
swerable without an explanation which is harder to accept
than the difficulty it seeks to explain.

> For this cause I also, *having heard* of the faith in the Lord
> Jesus which is among you, and the love which ye show toward
> all the saints, cease not to give thanks for you . . . (Eph. 1:
> 15-16.)

> For this cause I Paul, the prisoner of Christ Jesus in behalf of
> you Gentiles—*if so be that ye have heard of the dispensation
> of that grace of God which was given me to you-ward;* how
> that by revelation was made known unto me the mystery, as I
> wrote before in few words, *whereby, when ye read, ye can per-
> ceive my understanding in the mystery of Christ* . . . (Eph.
> 3:1-4.)

> But ye did not so learn Christ; *if so be that ye heard him, and
> were taught in him,* even as truth is in Jesus . . . (Eph. 4:20-
> 21.)

Thus, if the words "at Ephesus" (Eph. 1:1) are an original
part of the writing, we have a document not from Paul but
from a later writer who has sadly slipped in impersonating
Paul writing to a group of friends with whom he had been
long in the closest association. Its marked similarity with Colossians, far from being a guaranty of the genuineness of Ephesians (and precisely the same may be said for II Thessalonians, which is such a slavish copy of I Thessalonians,
save in the one key section so seemingly un-Pauline in tone) is

precisely the reverse. Not only is it difficult to see why Paul should have indulged in such laborious copying—he would not have needed to use such a means to make his writing seem Pauline, as a later falsarius well might—but not infrequently there are differences, subtle but real, in the meaning of the same phrase, which definitely raise one's suspicions. In both Colossians and Ephesians the figure of Christ as the "head" of the "body" occurs,[41] but with an amazing difference. According to Colossians, Christ is the head of the cosmic forces; the "world" is the body. In Ephesians, Christ is the head, and the church is the body. Arguments of this sort incline me against either the often-repeated contention of Ussher, that our Ephesians was a circular letter intended for several churches, or Marcion's identification of it as the otherwise missing letter to Laodicea. The chief argument for the genuineness of Ephesians has always been the difficulty to see just what the purpose of the falsarius was in writing this letter and ascribing it to Paul.

But before an attempt is made to answer that contention it may be said that the absence of a letter from Paul's pen to Ephesus is not surprising. When once he had reached that city, he seems to have made it his headquarters for several years. And when finally he left Ephesus for Macedonia, his feeling of being under the sentence of death was directed at the non-Christian populace, not at the church. Thus there would not seem to have been any occasion to have written these instructions, since he was always, during that extended period, within call. While at Corinth, if our contention regarding the nature of our Romans is correct, he did send a copy of that letter, with an added injunction regarding their cordial welcome of Phoebe, to the city so long his home, where, to borrow Arthur Nock's happy phrase, "he had founded a diocese and not a congregation." [42]

It has often been argued that while Paul caused a deal of stir during his lifetime he quickly dropped out of sight—at least for a period of years—after his death. The figure of speech has occasionally been suggested: he was a huge rock in the swiftly moving stream, causing the waters to divide; but once they had passed him, they united without a further trace. It was not till later, when "Luke" chanced to select him as the hero of his piece, that Paul was brought back to prominence. Then, once Acts had rehabilitated Paul, it was but a natural step that one of its readers, who himself knew that Paul had written at least an occasional letter, used the itinerary suggested in Acts as a vade mecum, revisited the churches therein mentioned as scenes of Paul's labors, made a collection of all the letters he could find, and published them. Thus Acts was the cause of the Pauline collection.

I am inclined to reverse this hypothesis. I see no evidence for this temporary eclipse of Paul. Rather, his death—especially if it was a martyr's death—heightened his fame and led to applause rather than to recrimination. Thus I would assume that the collection of Paul's letters (which are so evident in their influence upon the later writers, i.e., the authors of the seven Catholic Epistles and the author of the Revelation of John, with its curious inclusion, so unusual in an apocalypse, of the seven letters to the churches) was the incentive to, not the resultant of, the chronicle in Acts. These letters, now collected and, as we have seen, replete with hints from which a pretty full "life" can be hazarded, led Luke to write his provocative, if imaginative, account, utilizing all the hints Paul had left and skillfully toning down, or tuning out, the constant conflict which to Luke, now that the shouting and the tumult were long past, was not edifying or of a sort to be headlined. Why wash your dirty linen in public?

Are there any clues as to the reason for the first collection of scattered letters and the making of them available for all Christians? Is there any clue as to the identity of the man who did so epoch-making a service? I am inclined to think there is. Conspicuous among the letters is the charming little personal note to Philemon, urging the latter to receive back kindly his runaway slave Onesimus. It is a lovely little note, but hardly of world-shaking content. It does not demand or hint at the abolition of slavery. It raises no important questions, theological or otherwise. Why did it chance to be preserved?

To one man it was of prime importance, and that man was the slave whom Paul had met in prison, had converted, had befriended, and had sent back home with so gracious a note of support. We know from Ignatius' letter to Ephesus that, at the time he wrote, an Onesimus, "a man of inexpressible love" [43] was the bishop of Ephesus. Was he the same Onesimus? It is impossible to prove, but there is no obvious hindrance to the possible identification. Had he years before repaid the debt he owed to the now-dead Paul by visiting the churches and salvaging what he could find of letters from his patron? Surely he would not have needed any source like Acts to retrace Paul's steps. His time with Paul in prison had given him ample opportunity to learn the details of his hero's missionary work.

Having collected all the letters and pieces he could find, he had published them in collected form, not forbearing to include the note to Philemon, which had proved so dear to him. On an earlier page I mentioned the real problem which Ephesians poses. It cannot be a letter to Ephesus; it is unlikely to be a letter from Paul. Just what was its purpose? Unlike II Thessalonians, which has a definite ax to grind, and which uses I Thessalonians as the natural model; unlike the Pastorals, wherein the later Paulinist has many warnings to give against a very present trouble and ventures to do it humbly in the name of the great teacher he so admired—unlike these situations, there seems little to have spurred a later writer to activity, utilizing Colossians as a model.

But if the suggestion I am making is valid, that Onesimus was the one who had taken the stand,[44] and if, as Goodspeed [45] has so plausibly and persistently argued, the editor wished to preface his collection with an introduction, essentially a mosaic of all the genuine letters he had gathered, everything would fall into place. Onesimus, earlier a member of the church at Colossae, had long known that epistle. It would not be surprising if he modeled his introductory epistle after the one so long familiar to him. That there was anything dishonest or improper in his eyes in such an act is absurd. Rather, it was a lovely tribute to the man who had meant so much to him and other Christians.

Of course this hypothesis cannot be proved. It has the merit of satisfying all of the problems involved without undue violence. Onesimus, the Colossian, now an important figure in Ephesus, which seemingly became one of the really great Christian centers, renowned for its literary productions, would seem a most natural candidate for identification as the otherwise unknown editor, whose work has had a literally incalculable effect on all subsequent Christian thinking.

9 | CARE OF ALL THE CHURCHES

What his letters show

Paul's letters provide us with a wealth of material for reconstructing his fifteen or more years of ministry, in consequence of which we find well-established groups of Christians, for the most part of Gentile origin, established in cities and towns throughout what we now style the Near East. They give us vivid pictures of Paul himself, his absolute confidence in the truth of what he styled his gospel, a very clear indication of what that gospel was, of the various problems and perplexities which this new gospel provided for those to whom it was proclaimed by its tireless champion, and the way Paul sought to meet and answer their questions, uncertainties, and at times heated disclaimers.

Paul had not written the letters for the purpose of passing this information on to subsequent generations. For the latter he had no thought or concern. Actually, in his thinking there would be no such. His certainty that the return of Christ—the end of the present age, and the culmination of history which would eclipse all else—was soon to come: this would have been sufficient to make the thought of a word to later generations absurd. Seemingly, Paul never gave up that passionate confidence in the new age, soon to dawn, which had become his in consequence of his earlier fruitless attempts to contradict it when sounded by those who had inherited it from their

crucified but risen Lord. His words were not for later generations but for groups that he had been instrumental in establishing and for whom he felt a continued responsibility when
word reached him of their difficulties, at times when he was
momentarily unable to visit them and deal directly with the
peculiar problems involved.

That subsequently these letters, or some of them, were to be
collected and published was known to neither the author nor
his readers. That Paul had expected them to be destroyed
after a first casual reading is unlikely; compare his word to the
Colossians:

> And when this epistle hath been read among you, cause that
> it be read also in the church of the Laodiceans; and that ye
> also read the epistle from Laodicea. (Col. 4:16.)

But to think that he expected them to be read and prized as
Holy Scripture two thousand years later borders on the grotesque.

It is scarcely to be claimed that the word of Clement in
Rome to the Corinthian church—"Take up the epistle of the
blessed Paul the Apostle" (I Clem. 47:1)—proves that by the
time of Clement the letters of Paul had been collected and circulated. Clement's word does indicate that Paul's letter was
still in their possession. This in itself is sufficient to make the
probability real that they were, at least occasionally, consulted
and read, even if not as a regular part of church services, as
was later to be the case. That some of those known to us are
as they were when first received is unlikely. The condition of
the one we know as II Corinthians is informative. This writing, as has been argued repeatedly, would seem to be a conge-
ries of several letters, or their parts. Certainly chs. 10 to 13
would seem to be a sizable part of that stormy letter written
from Ephesus between our I Corinthians and chs. 1 to 7 of II
Corinthians. A good case can be made that II Cor. 6:14 to 7:1,
which so markedly seems an intrusion in its present position,

is a stray sheet from the first letter that Paul had written to Corinth, which he mentions in I Cor. 5:9 ff. Less certainly, but not impossibly, II Cor., chs. 8 and 9, have been regarded as one or more independent short notes. Thus it is quite possible that, when the collection was made, all Pauline material still available in the church's archives was gathered up. In addition to one letter, substantially as received (our I Corinthians), were fragments of other letters—some sizable, such as II Cor., chs. 1 to 7; another badly mutilated, with omissions, perhaps deliberately made to remove the more specific references, now pointless, to the leader of the opposition who had been belatedly repudiated by his fellows; a single stray sheet from the earlier "former letter." When gathered up by the later collector, it is scarcely surprising that shorter fragments were gathered together with more concern for preserving all the author's words than for their chronology. The oft-cited word by Polycarp in his letter to the Philippians, that Paul "when he was absent wrote letters to you, from the study of which you will be able to build yourselves up into the faith given you," [46] has raised questions as to the integrity of our one letter to the Philippians: at least it evidences, as does the cited word of Clement, that their preservation in the archives of the several churches had been due to their continued use, presumably in services of worship.

Although they are exclusively concerned with immediate problems and difficulties which had arisen in the several churches and are intended to correct such misunderstandings, they do provide vivid pictures of what may be styled "life in an early church" and of the basic emphases of the absent but concerned teacher. To repeat a warning already sounded: these letters were not replicas of Paul's initial instructions to the groups he was establishing. He had been with them, often for weeks and months, during which time it may be confidently assumed he had set forth in repeated detail "his gospel." Thus, to examine these letters as though they were complete texts, to be styled "What a young Christian needs to know," is as mistaken as is the other attempt to view them as ordered instruction to later generations.

While each letter shows different situations to which Paul felt constrained to reply, two major problems, always confronting him, appear fundamental: (1) the immediacy of the coming end of the present evil age, now dominated by Satan ("the god of this age [who] hath blinded the minds of the unbelieving"—II Cor. 4:4) and his evil angels;[47] (2) his insistence upon a life of severe morality, alone worthy of one in Christ.

In I Thessalonians, seemingly the first from his pen, both of these problems are to the fore. Not unnaturally, the contention that this present world was soon to disappear and that those approved by God were to be removed from it to a new realm to which the resurrected Jesus had already returned had a definitely unsettling effect. Were this to be the case, why should they continue to work? Why should not their fellows who chanced to have a bit of property turn this to practical use, for they could not take it with them? To this seemingly so natural a contention, Paul addresses himself without compromise or qualification and with no concern that logically it was eminently sensible. They were to quit this fevered nonsense, were to stop gadding about and unsettling their fellows, were to get to work. This attitude might well seem—and be—highly illogical, but it evidences the solid and wholesome common sense of a man whose feet were solidly on the ground: although he firmly believed the world was going to end on the morrow, he demanded a quality of life lived as if it would last forever.

Apparently in Thessalonica, between the time of Paul's departure and the word which reached him from this new church, one or more of the converts had died. Their friends were greatly disturbed by this, which to them was a tragic situation. Would not the dead be deprived of their part in the coming glory when the Lord returned? To answer the groundless fears of these "fainthearted," Paul's word is explicit:

But we would not have you ignorant, brethren, concerning them that fall asleep; that ye sorrow not, even as the rest, who have no hope. For if we believe that Jesus died and rose again, even so them also that are fallen asleep in Jesus will God bring with him. For this we say unto you by the word of the Lord, that we that are alive, that are left unto the coming of the Lord, shall in no wise precede them that are fallen asleep. For the Lord himself shall descend from heaven, with a shout, with the voice of the archangel, and with the trump of God: and the dead in Christ shall rise first; then we that are alive, that are left, shall together with them be caught up in the clouds, to meet the Lord in the air: and so shall we ever be with the Lord. Wherefore comfort one another with these words. (I Thess. 4:13-18.)

These words were no figure of speech which today needs to be demythologized. They set forth in precise terms what Paul expected actually to take place. Again it is to be insisted that Paul lived in the first century, not in the twentieth. What to us seems grotesquely unreal—although we still preserve it unchanged in some of the hymns and gospel songs, with the saving proviso, "It is true as poetry is true"—was to him sober and literal fact. Nor is this to be dismissed as an early fantastic notion soon modified or given up by Paul. Precisely the same belief is to be found in the apparently much later letter to Corinth:

Behold, I tell you a mystery: We all shall not sleep, but we shall all be changed, in a moment, in the twinkling of an eye, at the last trump: for the trumpet shall sound, and the dead shall be raised incorruptible, and we shall be changed. (I Cor. 15:51-52; cf. Rom. 13:11.)

One of the most real values from this vignette from the past is the light it throws on Paul. He had apparently amplified the picture of the coming event because of the unselfish concern of his friends: they were worried about the fancied loss to their deceased friends. Had their concern been for their own coming glory, it is highly probable that we would not have received this vivid description. Again and again, under a crabbed exterior, we glimpse a warmhearted and devoted friend.

The other problem which Paul constantly faced, namely, the unconcern in his Gentile churches for what in his eyes loomed so great, the necessity of scrupulous purity of life, is also found in I Thessalonians. Actually this letter, so typically Pauline, provides the best introduction to both him and his letters of all his epistles. For a well-rounded picture of Paul, here is the place to start. The letter is not intended for all Christians, not even for all Paul's converts. It is directed solely to those in this capital city of Macedonia, and its contents are severely limited to attempting to make complete what he sees is still lacking in their faith.

After a simple and unostentatious heading comes a paragraph of compliment and appreciation. Since most of his letters were intended to correct missteps which he deplored and were regularly very distinct and insistent in reproof, it is not surprising that they are regularly preluded by a word of affectionate intimacy and recognition of their strong points: he is not an outsider limiting himself to critical disparagement; rather he is a father who is pained by his children's errors, but aware of their points of strength. I doubt that Paul had ever read Cicero's prescription for the construction of the opening paragraph of a speech likely to be successful:

> Make your introduction of such a character that it will render your hearer favorably disposed to you, willing to be informed, and attentive.[48]

But Paul's down-to-earth realism and common sense led him regularly so to start his letters. Only in the case of Galatians is it omitted. As he starts that letter, written in a white heat of anger, he is apparently at a loss for anything for which to praise them; the change from "I thank my God always concerning you" to "I marvel that ye are so quickly removing" (Gal. 1:6) is revelatory.

But to return to I Thessalonians: after this natural start, Paul meets his enemies' charges, which have poisoned some of his converts and made them suspicious of him. This teacher, who had promised soon to return, instead had gone south to Athens and Corinth in seeming disregard of his promise. Then he turns to the weaknesses of some of the Thessalonians, shown by the report he had received, and urges purity of life, a quiet and helpful spirit of love, and an understanding and informed faith in the blessing of God, soon to be revealed, which will relieve the apprehensive fears of the folk for whom the death of their friends had raised theological doubts. This done, he ends his letter with a few general admonitions to harmony and good order.

The second problem which Paul faced was the bland indifference shown by so many of his Gentile converts to what was to him—in no small part due to his Jewish heritage, where ethics was indivisible from religion—of capital importance: namely, purity of life, especially in the sphere of sexual practice. The fight against sexual impurity was one in which he was constantly engaged. In many of the cults of the Oriental world the sexual life and religion were closely associated. It had been true in Hebrew history too, due to the involvement with Canaanite practices incident to the conquest of Canaan, in which the winner had gained but a Pyrrhic victory; the Hebrews had won the land but had been worsted by their defeated foes, whose ways of life and worship had been among the things taken over. But the Deuteronomic reform had closed that chapter, and the swing of the pendulum had been very pronounced. In the resultant Judaism, an uncompromising emphasis had been laid upon the purity of family life. This emphasis continued, so that in the days of Paul dereliction of this sort constituted one of the three cardinal sins, never to be committed, whatever the consequence. Thus, in the lists of vices to be resolutely avoided by those in Christ, Paul regularly cites first those connected with sexual relations: incest, adultery, fornication, and pederasty.[49]

In many of the more respectable of the cults in the Mediterranean world, the wildest of orgies often accompanied the ceremonies, though not part of the ritual. To all this the Gentile Christian was accustomed. He was inclined to regard such excesses or even deviations very leniently, if indeed he was not disposed to indulge in them himself. Unchastity in an *unmarried* daughter was a grievous wrong against her family, since it caused the daughter's marital chances to be lessened; but aside from that, it carried no particular disgrace or opprobrium. The word attributed to Demosthenes[50]—"Mistresses we keep for pleasure, concubines for the sake of daily intercourse, wives to bear us legitimate children and to be our faithful housekeepers"—would have seemed to many an obvious and normal remark. The attitude of some of Paul's converts at Corinth, in whose eyes unrestrained sexual acts were normal ("meat for the belly, the belly for meat") reflected an outlook advocated by some of the Cynics, of whom Diogenes was a striking example.

Against this Paul set his face resolutely. Marriage he recognized and approved, although in view of the near end of the age it might well involve sad loss and heartaches. It might conceivably divert the couple from the wholehearted devotion to the Lord which one freed from domestic responsibilities could offer, but for many, if not most, it was a wise and natural state. So his words to those in Thessalonica, whom he styled "the weak," presumably in reference not to doctrinal insufficiency but to what was, in Paul's eyes, their vicious life:

> God's will is this, that you be consecrated, that is, that you abstain from fornication, that each of you respect his own wife; that each of you get his own wife in the spirit of consecration and honour not in the passion of lust, as is the case with the Gentiles who know not God, to prevent any one of you from disregarding or taking advantage of his brother in the matter. For the Lord is an avenger for all these matters, as indeed we

have predicted and solemnly affirmed; for God has not called
us Christians for impurity but to be consecrated; consequently
the rejecter rejects not man but God who puts his Spirit, the
consecrating Spirit, into you.[51]

This clear-cut distinction, inherited from Judaism and ever
to the fore in Paul's code of conduct for his churches, was a
constant source of perplexity—at times, of protest—for his
churches. His insistence that sexual intercourse unblessed by
marriage was a grievous sin in the eyes of God had two
results: many Gentiles, alarmed by his warning and failing to
see the distinction—within or without the marital state—took
what seemed to them the safest course, namely, refraining
completely from such a seeming potential danger, and even
sought to end unions already made. Against such unwarranted
action Paul sounded his warning. While the unmarried state
was advantageous, for many it was impractical. Far better was
it to marry than to be a prey—and likely a victim—to unsat-
isfied lust. Nor were husbands and wives to separate. On the
Lord's authority, not his own (I Cor. 7:10), he insisted on the
indissoluble nature of the marriage relation. In cases where a
husband or wife had been converted while the other partner
had not—a situation peculiarly of the past, for, of course, no
Christian was to marry an unbeliever (cf. I Cor. 7:39)—the
union was not to be broken. The Christian need have no fear
of defilement through continuing to live with his heathen mate.
Should the unbeliever insist on separation, the Christian was
to allow it, for there was no certainty that the unbeliever
would be eventually converted. The chances were too slim to
risk the rancor and discord which might well result. God had
called them to peace, not strife (I Cor. 7:12-24).

Thus this insistence by Paul reveals not only his unlimited
hatred of sexual irregularity but also his practical common
sense. Laxity in matters sexual was the order of the day. If
now the impression became circulated that Christians who
were "free from the Law" were above the Law and hence

nothing they did was sinful—a position apparently taken by at least some of the "spirituals" in Corinth, but by no means limited to Corinth or even to past years—a riot of excess was certain, and the Christian name would suffer.

In the eyes of many of Paul's Gentile converts the matter seemed very different. This unnatural forbidding of all sexual union save between husband and wife was but one of the unnatural and perverse superstitions of the Jews, akin to forbidding the use of pork and demanding one day of laziness out of every seven. Paul was telling them that their union with Christ had freed them from the bondage of the law of Moses; yet in the same breath he was demanding their continued subjection to that from which he had said they were free. He was ever insisting that in their baptism the old sinful man had died and that, like Christ, they had been raised to a new life which was Spirit-filled and Spirit-directed. This they had done. As truly as the arrogant and heavy-handed Paul, they were "in Christ," guided and inspired by God's holy Spirit. Why then should he venture to lay these arbitrary demands upon them? Why should he insist that the peculiar sort of life which he himself professed, largely because he was a Jew born and bred, should be a hampering chain on the necks of those admittedly free? Who was Paul to insist that only the sort of life which he happened to approve was "worthy of one in Christ"?

Many have been the attempts to explain the heated opposition that Paul so often found among his converts—notably, but far from exclusively, in Corinth and Galatia—and frequently the attempts to reconstruct the situations and their causes have been both erudite and forced. It would appear to me that a far simpler and more probable explanation is so plainly evident that it tends to be overlooked or discarded in a fevered search for the more obscure and therefore, in "holy history," the more probable.

10 | THE GOSPEL ACCORDING TO PAUL

A well-rounded religion

By faith in Christ and the power of his resurrection the Christian came into immediate fellowship with his Lord. He was baptized into His death and, thus leaving behind his old sinful nature, was raised into newness of life. He had died to the flesh, characterized and dominated by all its lusts, and henceforth lived to the spirit. Thus he actually became a new man in Christ Jesus. He had been consecrated, set apart by baptism, but this rite, though important, did not have the same magical effectiveness as did the similar initiatory rites of the other cults. In them it was sufficient. By this initiation into the cult the devotee learned the secret by the aid of "the things done and the things said"; accordingly, salvation was unconditionally assured him. The Christian rite was in some measure similar, in that it too plunged the initiate into mystic union with the risen Lord, by the impartation of whose spirit a new life began; yet that was not all. His life must conform to his new exalted status of being "in Christ," that is, mystically and intimately united with the risen Christ. By this union he was assured a place in the eternal destiny of the world, in the new age soon to be ushered in. Death, should that come before the dawn of the new age, would have no effect save that of bringing the Christian into an even closer union freed from any danger of relapse into sin.

But this glorious destiny was only for those who actually lived "in Christ." To be sure, good works as such, keeping of the Law and the like, could not grant this boon; it must come as the free gift of God, to be appropriated by the Christian's faith; yet this faith was by no means a mere intellectual assent. It was not a creed, as it was to become in later years; it was a life—the new life which the man who had found fellowship with Christ lived in him. It was the new character he bore conformed to Christ's own. It made great demands, but it brought with it sufficient strength. As Matthew Arnold neatly expressed it:

> The surpassing religious grandeur of Paul's conception of faith is that it seizes a real salutary emotional force of incalculable magnitude, and reinforces moral effort with it.[52]

It was a new life where the flesh was in subjection to the spirit and brought forth fruits evidencing the fact that the man was righteous before God. For Paul, morality, far from being of little or no consequence, as it was for most of the other mysteries, was directly resultant from his doctrine of salvation through faith. The Christian was impelled toward a certain kind of life by virtue of his union with his Lord. If he was really consecrated, separate, set apart to God (Paul's word was *hagios*), to Paul's mind he must inevitably show it; if he was really yoked to Christ, he must live in a fitting way. The exalted position that the Christian held was actually "in his Lord," and with his Lord dwelling in him (phrases not to be considered figures of speech but to be understood literally). Christ—not Jesus of Nazareth, but the everliving Son of the Father—actually entered the man, set him free, brought him from death to life, and would not fail to bring him to the full stature of the perfect man:

> In Christianity a character conformed to God's own is the consequence of the grace of God in Jesus Christ, through the Holy

Spirit. The possession of such a character is therefore the cri-
terion of the genuineness of man's faith and the reality of his
union with Christ.[53]

This was the gospel which Paul was sure he had been called
to preach. It was at once his duty and his joy to make it
known to all men. He was not ashamed of it, for it was the
power of God to salvation to all who accepted it. His task was
to strive in every possible way to offer this gospel to men that
they would accept it; that he might present all men faultless in
Christ Jesus; that at the great day of judgment, when all men
stood before the judgment bar (II Cor. 5:10; Rom. 14:10), it
might be not a day of wrath (Rom. 2:5), but a day of salvation (II Cor. 6:2). To attain this he would go to all extremes.
Though free through the power of Christ's death, he gladly
made himself a slave to all that he might win all for Christ.
Though a free man, he rejoiced that he was privileged to be
Christ's slave in that glorious task. Nothing else in life
counted: the most prized possessions of life—high rank, a
noble ancestry, a rich heritage—of which he had been proud,
he now gladly reckoned as less than nothing. In comparison
with this one great hope of being found in Christ, and through
a life of participation in Christ's sufferings of attaining to the
resurrection of his Lord, they were but refuse and offscouring
(Phil. 3:4 ff.).

This was the heritage in store for every Christian. The prize,
beside which all else was worthless, was the call to this glorious fellowship which came from God through Christ Jesus
(Phil. 3:14). The way might be rough; the Christian life,
which must be resolutely achieved, might be accompanied by
suffering; temptations would come, but never beyond their
strength (I Cor. 10:13); false teachers would strive to deceive;
the lusts of the flesh would menace: all these must be crushed.
The struggle would be desperately hard, but the goal would
be worth it. Nor must they wait too long. The day was at
hand. For those who failed, it would be a day of wrath and

condemnation; but to those who were in Christ, and whose lives proved it, it would be a day of praise and honor, and, better than that, of eternal life in and with their Lord. Thus the first demand upon a Christian was, as an individual, to make his life conform to that of his Lord; to cut himself free resolutely from all that would hinder and impede. Its character was purity, separateness; its motive the hope of eternal salvation.

To us today Paul's emphasis on morality and his insistence that actual union with Christ must result in a changed life seem perfectly normal. It must not be overlooked—to repeat a point constantly stressed—that such would not have been the consensus in his own day. The Oriental mystery cults made no such demands on their devotees; correctness of ritual, not purity of life, was the essential requirement. Moreover, religion and ethics in the ancient world were not so nearly identified as we are wont to make them today, due in no small degree to our heritage from Judaism, made insistent by Paul.

This makes the more noteworthy Paul's insistence on the changed life that bears fruits of the Spirit, for one might expect from a word such as Rom. 11:6 ("But if it is by grace, it is no more of works: otherwise grace is no more grace"), where faith and works are set in seeming contrast, that Paul would have disagreed utterly with James. Here Paul and James, however, are on entirely different ground. It is quite in error to feel that one has a broader view than the other, for they are not discussing the same matter. James is arguing that both faith and works are necessary; Paul, on the contrary, although setting fully as high an ethical standard, denies that salvation comes through works, but insists that the deeds evidence the fact that the individual has actually entered into union with Christ, this made possible by God's demanding call. Paul would not have quarreled with James's contention about morality or the necessity of works, although he would probably have preferred to call the latter "fruits of the Spirit." The important fact, too often overlooked, is that what Paul

stigmatized as "works of the law" are by no means the same as
the works which the Epistle of James demands, while the sort
of faith which James calls "dead" would never have been
classed as faith at all by Paul.

The point of importance in seeking to know the apostle to
the Gentiles is not to strive to defend his logic—always a
difficult, at times an impossible, undertaking—but to recognize
how fundamental to all his thinking was the emphasis on
moral probity. Well did he realize the danger of his emphasis
on freedom from law. Those who styled themselves "spiritual"
(*pneumatikoi*) at Corinth were evidencing the results that
might well come from such a teaching when, detached from
moral requirements, liberty easily emerges as license. Accordingly, again and again he asserts that such conduct clearly revealed the fact that the faith professed was not in Christ but
in the power of wickedness, and warns that all men, regardless
of baptism, must stand before the judgment bar. Occasional
words (notably Rom. 14:10; II Cor. 5:10; I Cor. 3:13 ff.)
would seem to give some justification for considering that Paul
felt that, though all would be searched and proved, and that
the one whose works failed the test would suffer a grievous loss,
yet he would be ultimately saved. On the one hand, faith must
be a new life; fruits of the Spirit must be shown. Baptism and
being *hagios* were not enough. On the other hand, the man
brought into union with Christ, even though he grievously
fails, has been baptized and will be saved (cf. I Cor. 5:5).
The two cannot be reconciled.

The question has often been raised why Paul laid the stress
he did on moral conduct. Some—especially those who tend to
view him as a "Hellenistic Jew of the Diaspora"—have seen a
Stoic influence at work in the apostle. There is no question but
what Stoic moral requirements were strict in Paul's time and
that he would have approved them, but I see no reason for assuming influence when the evidence is lacking. Paul's heritage
from Judaism is sufficient to explain his attitude.

In Judaism, religion and morals were essentially identified,

and the highest of standards for conduct were set. God had revealed his will in requirements of conduct as in everything
else. Israel was to follow it. The fundamental requirement was
conformity to God: "My good man, the best of all prayers, and
the end and proper object of happiness, is to attain to a like-
ness of God." [54] "Be ye holy; for I am holy." (Lev. 11:44.)
Whatever the original meaning of that ancient word may have
been, it had come to indicate a God of unstained character.
No impure myths or legends were told of his amours. He was
a God of righteousness and of holiness. And holiness—at least
in the days of Judaism (due, as has already been remarked, in
no small part to the sweeping reform of the Deuteronomic
purge)—signified moral purity. Accordingly, the people must
reflect this character in their lives.

Paul held this view of God. This moral outlook on life was
bred in the bone. So when he came to his view of the mystical
union of the believer with Christ—which lay at the bottom of
all his thinking and was the direct, if developed, consequence
of the revelation he had received in Damascus—it was but
natural that the same moral requirements should be made.
Christ was no unmoral or immoral deity, as were the lords of
some of the other mystery cults. None of the amours or impure
stories that were told of all the pagan deities were told of him.
His character was of the same spotless purity as was that of
Yahweh. As a result, requirements of character, often neglected or unnoticed by the ministrants of the Oriental cults,
were of prime importance to Paul. Such was the Lord to
whom Christians were most intimately united, who dwelt in
them, and to whom they were set apart from all that would
defile. Anything that would tend to sully Christ, to join him to
a harlot, to defile the body which was his holy temple, was an
abomination and to be shunned resolutely.

The historian is always subject to the danger of attempting
to find the complete explanation of a man in his environment
and heritage, and thus of neglecting the personal element. In
none is this more unfortunate than in Paul. He was a debtor

both to Jew and to Greek, but this does not explain him. His own personality and individual contribution cannot be neglected. This is particularly true in his moral teaching which, unlike his theology, never seems forced or struggling. Here Paul is reflecting his own outlook on life. He can well admonish his churches to become imitators of him. Often he has been charged with being both a casuist and an opportunist, but the criticism neglects the essential fact that his opportunism was never for his own advantage. He might be all things to all people, but his purpose was to win them for God.

Philippians 1:15-18 is instructive. Apparently some Christians who were jealous of Paul had been striving to undermine his influence at Philippi and had made false charges against him. Paul refuses to yield to any personal animosity, but instead rejoices in so far as they preach Christ, in spite of their attacks upon him. This is one of the brightest spots in Paul's writings. No bidding for flattery here. His words reveal the sincerity and disinterested nature of the apostle's work. Or again in the delightful little letter to Philemon, which seems genuine if any of our letters are to be attributed to Paul, once more he shows his ethical soundness. Gladly would he have kept Onesimus to help him; yet he sends him back to make restitution, but with a letter from Paul urging his owner to exhibit Christian charity to the repentant runaway.

Paul was a practical man, and he realized that this was a practical world. Though the Christian was united with his Lord, he was also in the closest contact with his fellows. They had had similar experiences, were joined in the same vital union—or should be—with their risen Lord. Their tasks were much the same. Accordingly, they should live in the most perfect harmony, and by a mutual give-and-take strengthen each other in their glorious faith. Paul loves to emphasize the "solidarity" of man, the joint interest which, binding humanity together, makes the brother's interest truly one's own.

Here Paul made his most lasting contribution. The Stoics had urged a noble life, a resolute uprooting of all passions and appetites, a purging of the self from all excesses and lusts of the flesh, a daily self-examination and gradual improvement. But they failed conspicuously to provide a goal attractive to the many. Comparatively few people cared to accept the rigorous self-discipline with no goal save doing it because it was right, noble though this insistence truly was. Weariness in well-doing was the great obstacle. There was no future reward held out to them, nor was there a challenging social call to do it for the sake of one's fellow citizen.

Paul met both those longings. As did the other mystery cults, Christianity promised its adherents future life where all transient sufferings would be forgotten in the glorious estate reserved for them. And Christianity was, to repeat, free from the extravagances and obscenities which too often marred the other mysteries and had to be explained or allegorized away. But in addition to this goal or result, which served as a tremendous motive, Paul gave Christianity a lasting solidarity by his constant emphasis on their obligations one to the other. Not only was a man to strive to walk worthily of the inheritance that was to be his, and by his purity of life to show that he was a "new man"; but he was to live and act in such a way that his brother might also attain. They were a little band of people, sojourners in a foreign land. Heaven was their home. They were exposed to dangers from both Jews and heathen. False brethren were striving to spy out their freedom, to bring them again into captivity to sin. They must offer an unbroken front to the enemy.

Nor was this the only reason for their union. Aside from the dangers from without that united them, Christians were to live together as brethren. Their faith was in a common Lord. Dissension and discord among themselves was a sin against Christ, for by the particular nature of their bond with him they were linked together. As Christ dwelt in them, they together actually formed his body, various members surely, but yet actually making up the body. Lack of harmony, factiousness, and the like would disrupt Christ's body; so the sin of the one was against the many. The consciousness of the corporate life, of the unity of believers, was the most effective motive that Paul could have urged upon his fellow Christians for achieving the true fellowship (*koinōnia*).

Love and forbearance were the great social virtues. Love that united all in the common bond, that saw in one's neighbor's good his own: this was the social virtue par excellence. It stood as the fulfillment of all law (Rom. 13:8-10; Gal. 5:14). But complementing it was forbearance. If Christian groups were to be in harmony and peace—and God had called them to peace (I Cor. 7:15; cf. also Rom. 14:19)—they must show forbearance each to the other. As each had received special gifts from God, he was to use them, but was to remember that the really great gifts were those that ministered to the edification of all. All had not reached the same stage of moral maturity. Those who were strong must never misuse their freedom; rather, they were to bear the burdens of the weak (Rom. 15:1), lest the weaker brother perish—a brother for whose sake Christ had died (I Cor. 8:11). On the contrary, it is to be noted, the weaker brother is not to relapse into self-complacency on account of his scruples and to assume a self-righteous judgment toward those who have more common sense. "Let not him that eateth not judge him that eateth: for God hath received him." [55] As love was the all-enduring virtue and forbearance was its corollary, service was the great duty. Each man was to help the other; service was the law of life. They had been called to freedom—not, however, to a freedom that was license, but where love found its expression in service (Gal. 5:13).

In such a group, arrogance and pride would be out of place. They were not their own but were bought with a price; their status was that of sons, no longer slaves, and was not a reward achieved by their own merits of which they could afford to boast. It was a gift to them from God. Each was to walk preferring his neighbor to himself and in obedience to those in spiritual authority over them. Thus the purity and uprightness, the strictness and temperance of life that was demanded of the individual Christian as such from his relation to Christ flowered out into the social virtues and duties, due to the fact that all were members one of another, making up the body of Christ.

But though the Christians were thus united through their Lord one to another, they were living in a hostile world. Accordingly, questions arose as to what should be the relation of the individual Christian and of the Christian fellowship with the world. Paul's teaching was explicit. To the government and those in authority over them they were to be in the most lawful obedience, for the powers that be were ordained by God (Rom. 13:1-7). To the members of the world they were to be discreet; all fellowship with them was not forbidden, indeed could not be. Christians lived in the world, although they were not of the world (I Cor. 5:9-13). They were to be ever conscious, however, of the difference between themselves and those about. If the Christian was the slave of a heathen master, he was to serve him in the most perfect fidelity. If a Christian was married to an unbeliever, the Christian was not to seek to break the alliance unless the unbeliever so insisted. But he was not to make new alliances of this sort. So far as possible he was to remain unfettered. The attitude seems to be expressed by the warning: Be discreet, avoiding everything that would subject the Christian fellowship to attack or defamation. Various questions presented themselves and received special attention, but this seems the general principle underlying the apostle's advice.

Paul had no formal system of ethics, attempted no textbook for Christian conduct, though the *Haustafeln* ("household duties") in Colossians[56] might seem a step toward filling that need.[57] To repeat once more, ethics and religion for him, as for any other Jew, could not be dissociated. The Christian ethic was the living in a manner worthy of the high calling to which the Christian had been called. It embraced the whole of life and all its relationships. While occasional questions would arise as to the proper course to be followed with fellow Christians, with the group as such, or with unbelievers, yet the real answer was implicit in the Christian's proper conduct of life as such. Accordingly, all these distinctions which to a degree seem necessary for a modern consideration are not completely happy, and are not to be regarded as hard and fast. All the duties and virtues, the responsibilities and privileges, were included in the task the Christian had of living in a way worthy of his calling, and were inspired by the longing to attain his promised reward.

Throughout the epistles the ethical note is prominent. Theological or doctrinal discussions may engage Paul for the moment, yet, as Percy Gardner acutely observed many years ago in a volume still worth careful reading, he ever turns back "with obvious relief . . . to his ethical exhortation." [58] These exhortations for the most part were called forth to meet the specific needs of the Christians to whom he ministered, and thus were intensely practical and timely in their nature and are a far step from the ordered sequence of a Greek moralist like Aristotle. Yet they were not the impromptu words of an opportunist, but were the expression of the deep-seated principles governing his life—of the facts and implicates of union with Christ, and their corollary, the union of fellow believers in Christ. We might almost say this sense of *koinōnia* produced his ethics or at least gave to it its distinctive and timeless form.[59]

11 | AVE ATQUE VALE

A retrospect

That Paul has proved to be the most influential figure in the history and development of Christianity would not be a difficult thesis to support. During those early formative years, not only did he establish churches in strategic centers in the Roman world, but he kept in contact with these groups, not only in person but through letters. These letters were preserved, at least in substantial part, and soon came to be regarded as the common property of all Christians everywhere, eventually becoming a considerable part of what has come to be known as the New Testament. Not only that; these letters were responsible for the production of the other writings now bound with them in this Christian canon. They led directly to the production of the seven we know as General Epistles, were certainly an impetus for the parallel production of letters and other writings we know as the Apostolic Fathers, and to no small degree were influential in the production of the first five books—the four Gospels and Acts—in our present New Testament. They were directly responsible for the activity of Marcion, whose work, however heatedly decried and attacked, was of direct consequence in the emergence of both a Christian canon and an organized and united Christian church.[60] They were of central importance to Augustine, Luther, and Calvin, whose combined influence on the development of

Christian history few would be disposed to question. Thus to deny the word "influential" to one who has wielded such a sway is impossible.

It is equally clear that the other descriptive adjective, "popular," has never been his. To his own churches he seemed both heavy-handed and dominating. To Jewish Christians, who in the early years considered themselves the core of the movement, he was a dangerous figure, blind to central values and but a Johnny-come-lately. To the Roman authorities in the cities and territories in which he labored he was a trouble-maker and a nuisance, if not worse. Nor is he much more favorably regarded today. To many—probably the bulk of those who wear at least nominally the appellation Christian—his is no inconsiderable part of the Bible, and so, of course, he must be accorded respect, but with little affection and quite destitute of anything approaching the sentimental acclaim showered on Jesus, especially at such seasons as Christmas and Easter. Occasional words and passages—notably I Cor. ch. 13, and Phil. 2:5-11—are widely acclaimed, despite the growing confidence of many literary critics that neither of these passages is more than a lovely piece which Paul utilized without acknowledgment. To be sure, professional students of early Christian history and literature are devoting much time and thought to his writings, but for the most part seemingly with more interest in trying to solve puzzles than in enjoying fellowship with the puzzle maker.

One of the reasons for this "unpopularity," which seems a realistic, if hesitant, description, is that all our sources of knowledge of him are from his own pen, and in no small part they seem repellent. Luke could use them, as I have suggested, but did not find them quotable; instead, without hesitation, he rewrote them.

In the case of Jesus the situation is very different. We have nothing from his own pen and very little of what can be realistically styled unaltered material. Instead we have encomiums and eulogies. The first three Gospels seem simple and easy to understand; the Fourth Gospel takes this simple figure, friend of the common people, ever going about to do good, and dresses him in robes of stained-glass grandeur. Whether this resultant dressed-up figure would have the same charm were it not for the fact that unconsciously we carry over to it and read into it the very different figure in Matthew, Mark, and Luke, is highly questionable. What we like is the combination.

All this is absent when we turn to Paul, especially to the chapters which usually stand in the forepart of his letters. In most of those chapters, of clarity there is little, of simplicity there is none. Instead there is much that warrants the word of the later writer: ". . . some things hard to be understood, which the ignorant and unstedfast wrest . . . unto their own destruction" (II Peter 3:16). In no small part this is due to the fact that Paul has been turned (actually this word may quite properly be emended to "forced") into a theologian, and in this transformation many of the crystal-clear, practical, down-to-earth, and eternally abiding emphases have been lost sight of. Instead we see the long, often turgid, arguments, cluttered with supposedly buttressing quotations, which often seem to warrant precisely the opposite conclusion than the one painfully reached.

At times I am reminded of the years when, as a student in graduate school in need of money, I tutored high school students lost in algebra. Frequent was the paper I sought to correct and understand. The first equation was correct; the second properly grew from it; likewise the fourth from the third: then came a strange confusion. It was impossible to see how equation five grew from four. But once that hurdle was made all became clear. Six was the proper consequence of five, and the next, viz., "$x = 7$," was manifestly correct. The solution was evident. The youngster had a table of answers. After he had gone as far as he could, he stopped and started to work backward, using the answer. Precisely the same is to be seen with Paul. He knew the answer he wished to reach—and he reached it.

Small wonder that in the eyes of many he "muddied the lim-
pid and clear waters of the gospel," the words of Jesus, with
his unwarranted complications. Thus the real Paul, amazingly
able to weld together groups of men and women, to give them
a solid and established foundation on which to stand, has been
too often lost sight of. Many of his views—notably his passionate certainty of the near approach of the catastrophic end of
the age—are fantastic in our eyes and have been proved by
the sober story of history to have been incorrect. But the same
must be said for Jesus, from whom he had inherited the view
which history has demonstrated to be wrong. For Jesus it
seems to have eclipsed all else. The one great desideratum was
admission to the "kingdom" when it dawned, as speedily it
would. This was seemingly the background for his insistences,
which have too often been examined and approved quite
apart from the need for them as he saw it. Thus we have such
demands, not alone in the Sermon on the Mount but throughout the Gospels, which are not merely unadapted for practice
in any nation, but which would, if adopted, result in euthanasia
of that state or nation. Not to resist evil is to give victory to
evil. This has been frequently seen in a Tolstoy or Brook
Farm. It could result only in the end of the proper possession
of property, of civil organization, even of domestic life. The
world has seen many such societies living solely for the ideal,
living a purely parasitic life: societies wandering, homeless, not
possessing property but content to live on the alms of the
faithful; not resisting evil but turning the other cheek—not in-
frequently that of wife or child—when the first has been un-
warrantably slapped; intent solely on learning and practicing
the (to them) clear "will of God."

This indifference, seemingly so central for Jesus, to such
matters as property or rule, due to his regarding them as passing (or, at least, inconsequential) trivia and of a sort to blind
the eyes to the one and only great necessity in view of the
fast-approaching kingdom, was fanatic and is of value only
when allegorized or spiritualized away. This rarified air—

"oxygen" some have styled it—must be tempered to the lungs of normal men and women, whose work makes possible the parasitic class able to practice nonresistance and all that goes with it. The great principles which seemingly, if life is to go on, are essential: love to God and man, unselfishness, kindness, and the like—these must be put in another setting. To continue the figure, this oxygen must be diluted by nitrogen and be made fit for the lungs of living men and women.

It is precisely here that Paul's ethics—unlike the apparently insolvent, if not irresponsible, emphasis of Jesus—is adapted to a settled society, as is ours today. It is not of the sort suited solely to wandering bands of enthusiasts able to exist only because some of their fellows by work and devotion give them what they decry but demand. Laws of marriage, property, almsgiving, obedience to law, readiness to work, understanding insistence on the responsibilities as well as the rights both of themselves and of others: these are and must be on a durable basis. Disregard of them is not only unrealistic but definitely wrong and to be resisted to the uttermost. Paul, like Jesus, may have thought that the world was going to end on the morrow, but he lived and taught, as I have constantly insisted, as if it would last for ever. Thus with very real profit we may reread his words, with an eye open to their frequency and import for the writer himself, and with a prayer of thanksgiving for the one who never wearied of so insisting.

To me it is increasingly apparent that the central note in Paul's instruction and the mainspring of his thinking is to be seen in a short phrase in one of his letters to Corinth: "For the love of Christ constraineth us (II Cor. 5:14). In these half dozen words, written nearly two millennia ago, is an insight into life which is timeless. The rallying call which has been raised in every age to enlist recruits for a new rebellion has been "Freedom!" The sound of the breaking of shackles—so deafening today—has come to be considered the very essence of the heavenly music. And each emancipation has been heralded abroad as the veritable prelude to the millennium. Yet as the historian looks back over the long story of what men have been pleased to call "civilization," he can hardly refrain from assent to the weary word of the greatest of the Hebrew prophets: "They have healed also the hurt of my people slightly, saying, Peace, peace; when there is no peace" (Jer. 6:14). The bars of wood have been broken, one after the other, only to be replaced by stouter bars of iron. In this pathetic and fruitless groping for a freedom which is as constantly elusive as a will-o'-the-wisp it is high time to raise the question whether the game is worth the candle. Is freedom to be found by those who seek for her? Has not the story of the years made one thing clear: there are cords about us, so intricately tied that to seek to break them serves to draw them but the tighter? Might it not be wiser to cease our fruitless quest of an imaginary something about which everyone seems to know everything except the means of finding it, and instead to raise the question: Since on every hand constraints and bonds are to be found, is it not conceivable that they are but a part of the eternal nature of life, and that removal would be fatal, as Aylmer discovered when he erased the birthmark on the cheek of his beloved Georgiana?

When we raise that question, these words of Paul, "The love of Christ constraineth us," speak with new meaning and insistence. If any words are to be spoken of as divinely inspired, these are of that number. They give expression to the paradox of life: We are free only because we are slaves. We can hold, only because we ourselves are held. There are rules in the game of life that cannot be broken.

This note was central for Paul. He could cry aloud in ringing defiance, "Am I not free? Am I not an apostle?" (I Cor. 9:1)—but only because the vision of Christ which had been his had brought the complementary truth that he was henceforth the slave of the one who had set him free.

These words, "The love of Christ constraineth us," take us to the very center of his thinking. Too often their significance has been missed. Countless attempts have been made to understand what Paul meant by the phrase, "the love of Christ." In technical grammatical parlance, it has been hotly debated whether "Christ" is here a subjective or an objective genitive. Is it the love which Christ has for us, or is it the love which we have for Christ? In my judgment both answers fall short of the real solution, which is far profounder. The love of Christ which constrains, dominates, masters, not only Paul but every Christian, is neither our love for Christ nor his for us, but it is a love, boundless in its scope, that is made possible as the Christian becomes identified with his Lord. In a word, it is the Christ-love.

To understand this as Paul did, we must recognize that for him the heart of the gospel lies in the word "in Christ." It was by faith in Christ and the power of his resurrection that the Christian came into immediate fellowship with his risen Lord. He was baptized into His death, and thus, leaving behind his old sinful nature, was raised into newness of life. But this new life he no longer lived alone. As a result of this experience a mystic change had taken place; as he had been crucified with Christ, so now Christ lived in him. The new man was thus actually a Christ-man. The words "in Christ" or "Christ liveth in me" are accordingly not to be understood as being figures of speech. Paul meant them to be understood literally. Thus "faith" did not mean for Paul an intellectual assent to notions, however valuable they might be. To a measured degree, "conviction" approaches the truth; yet actually it too falls short. The best understanding of what faith meant for Paul is reached by substituting for it the phrase "new life." The faith of the Christian was the new life he was living in Christ; the life Christ was living in him; better yet, the new life that was being lived by the newborn Christ-man.

This key opens many doors in Paul's writings that have too often seemed barred. Paul speaks of having the mind of Christ (I Cor. 2:16; cf. Phil. 2:5). What does he mean? To the man who actually is in Christ the new life is revealed in such a manner that he feels and finds himself impelled to it. He is so completely linked to Christ that he is no longer able to distinguish between his own desires and goals and those of his Lord. The distinction, in fact, no longer exists. He has the mind of Christ, not because he thinks as Christ thinks, but because Christ is actually thinking in him. His words are really Christ's own. Christ speaks through him.

Against this background, Paul's word, "The love of Christ constraineth us," takes on new meaning. The love of Christ is thus the Christ-love, the new outlook on life that has resulted from the believer becoming identified with his Lord. Because Christ himself—the complete and thus completing revelation of God—is love, there streams over Paul from communion with him this power of love as the motive power of all ethical action, of life itself. Thus the very sign of his freedom is the sign of his bondage. There can be no halfway measure or compromise. It is not so much a constraint from without as from within; it is nonetheless a constraint. The man who professes to be a new man, to be in Christ, and yet who resists this compelling wave of power, is a living lie; he is not in Christ at all, for, if he were, not only would he not be able to resist, but he would not wish to. Those faculties which could exercise such a desire would be no longer alive.

At once the chilling voice of logic makes itself heard. Paul, we say, is riding two horses at the same time. Why, if this divine economy of faith prevails, does he concern himself further with those who have become converts? Why give ethical admonitions to those who are faltering? How *can* they be faltering? It was precisely at this point, as has already been noted, that many of his converts raised their protests. Here was, and is, the age-old dilemma: theory and practical experience. Logically, of course, his admonitions and sharply defined rules of conduct were unnecessary, as many Corinthians heatedly protested. He who was in the Spirit would have supplied by the Spirit all necessary insight and help; would feel himself borne along on the great current streaming from Christ. And many were the converts who felt this keenly and resented Paul's heavy hand of constraint.

Yet all about him on every side Paul saw fellow Christians whose conduct he strongly disapproved. Thus by precept and example he sought to help and encourage those who, while in Christ, were yet babes in Christ. The fallacy is obvious and cannot be explained away. "Logic is at times," as someone (not improbably a theologian, hard pressed by his critics) has remarked, "only the hoop about little vessels to keep them from expanding." Its breach in Paul, it would almost seem, is what endears him most to those who have come to know him.

Even in his own day Paul was not understood. His insistence on freedom from the Law was understood, or at least accepted, as if it meant license; his teaching of faith—a new life with all its demands and consequences—came to be understood as the acceptance of dogmas divorced from conduct, and aroused the protest of a James. Nor has he fared much better in subsequent generations. From a man whose own life was a glowing example of the mystic truth he sought, at times laboredly, to preach, who, under the constraint of the Christ-love, gave himself in a world which had at best little desire for him, he has been transformed into the sinister figure who muddied the clear waters of the preaching of Jesus and who has been so dreadfully responsible for the warping and transforming of Christianity that we hear so much about today.

Many of the problems which convulsed him have solved themselves. Many others have arisen of which he never dreamed. His rugged, almost stubborn, honesty; his hatred of sham; his conviction that as an instrument of God, unworthy though he might have been, he must speak the truth as it was (that is, as God had given it to him and was compelling him to speak it)—these qualities sometimes offend us as they did his first hearers, for he gave body blows, he did not box as one beating the air. Nonetheless, far from being a liability either to modern Christianity or to more inclusive modern thought, he stands as one of its greatest assets. We may have to translate his ideas as well as his language, but his basic insight revealed and gave expression to some of the profoundest truths of life, which never wax old.

The difficulty we find today in grasping and making real the significance of Paul's basic conception, "in Christ," is evidenced by our fondness for giving it a figurative interpretation. This, as I have repeatedly suggested, appears to me far from Paul's intent. Living in the thought world of the first century, familiar with—if scornful of—many other cults, each with its lord with whom the worshiper not only came into contact, but actually became identified, Paul found no difficulty in the representation of such a relation between Christ and Christian.

For us there is an obvious difficulty. We may say "Christ"; we think "Jesus." And for the most orthodox Christian it is difficult, if not actually impossible, to conceive himself as being *in* Jesus of Nazareth. For Paul that difficulty did not exist. Christ was the eternal Son of the Father, his complete and all-inclusive revelation. To be sure, he had lived in human form for a short while; that, however, was but one phase of his real life. For us the "Life of Christ" means the career of the prophet from Nazareth; for Paul it meant the reality and lordship of the risen one. In a word, for Paul the "life of Christ" was not the life his first followers remembered, the months prior to his death. Rather, it was the life which followed this minor, if not inconsequential, interlude; that is, the present, unending life of the Son of God. This difference of emphasis may well account in no small measure for the seeming disregard Paul showed for the activity of the prophet by Galilee's lake. For us it is "Jesus whom God raised from the tomb"; for Paul it was "Christ and him crucified." And we tend to think, when we read this Pauline phrase, of the human Jesus, of his life of devotion and service, and from these we move on to the cross. For Paul it was seemingly the reverse. His thought is of the risen, exalted Christ whom God had revealed to him in that cataclysmic moment of rebirth in Damascus. His thought starts with this risen and exalted Christ and moves backward to the cross. As it moves back to the cross, Paul's attention is stayed by the crucifixion. This epitomizes completely the theological significance and deathless import of Christ's mission.

It was in this death that he had provided the means of man's transformation. Thus the Christian, in the last analysis, was not losing his identity in a historical figure, however exalted; rather he was, with his fellow believers, comprising the body of the Lord of life. And this conviction appears to me, with very little adaptation, to be not only possible but the real hope of Christianity today. The history of mankind has been the story of men and women striving to keep open the channels into their own lives from the source of true life itself. Again and again there have been moments in time when men have felt that in this individual or that, an especial influx of this life—many prefer to call it God—has been present. For Christians, Jesus of Nazareth has occupied that position. In him men have seen and continue to see all that they have been able to conceive a God could be. "He that hath seen me hath seen the Father" (John 14:9) is not likely as a historical word of Jesus; it is the repeated verdict of men looking back to find the embodiment of their dreams and the certainty of their reality. We call him Jesus, but we mean the source of strength to weak and faltering hands, the breath of life to fevered and discouraged hearts. We are fortunate indeed that our early brethren painted such a portrait that, when we view it, the additional lenses we must use do not make it seem grotesque.

The sense of oneness with that which stands secure, of union with a never-failing life: that is what we need today—the confidence that though our reservoirs are but small they are linked to a never-diminishing sea. When translated into such terms, the ancient word of Paul appears to me the sole hope for disillusioned, discouraged man.

But such a confidence, such a status, brings its own tremendous obligations. This Paul realized. This Christ-love, this union with the Lord of life, constrains, masters. In simplest terms, "The love of Christ constraineth us" can be adequately rendered "I must." We hold, but we are held. There is

no room for childish prattling about liberty and freedom.
When God was pleased to reveal his Son to Paul, the latter
was no longer free. From then on he was a slave. Woe was
him if he did not preach. The hand of constraint was ever
upon him. It drove him over weary miles, subjected him to the
gravest perils and most uncongenial men. Yet through the recognition of what he now was, all that might have been distasteful glowed in a new light. His hands might be chained;
his heart was aflame. His life was no longer a disorganized
one, where he must seek to pick and choose, fearful lest his
choice be unwise and that he find himself again fighting God
when he thought he was doing God service. The fact that he
found himself loving the things which God loved was proof
positive, and the peace that was now his in the place of doubt
and uncertainty was indicative that he stood in right relation
with God (cf. Rom. 5:1). No longer need he strive to kick
against the maddening goad. He was conscious that, though
he *must* do this, *must not* do that, there was nothing detri-
mental to his dignity in this servitude. His stigmata as Christ's
slave were the badges of his dignity as God's free man.

As I remarked on an early page, fifty years ago as I ap-
proached the Pauline letters, I was not attracted. As I became
better acquainted with Paul my feelings underwent a diamet-
ric reversal. He was the subject of my first book. It seems to
me only proper that he is the subject of what may be my last.
As I read his letters, the word of early Christianity's nameless
scholar about Abel's sacrifice appears to me most fitting for
these letters: "through them he being dead yet speaketh" (cf.
Heb. 11:4). When many years ago I first read Tacitus' word of
appreciation of his father-in-law Agricola, it seemed to me a
lovely tribute and one hard to surpass. I would appropriate it
gratefully in love and appreciation of one long to me a deeply
revered friend and elder brother:

> *Quicquid ex Paulo amavimus, quicquid mirati sumus, manet
> mansurumque est in animis hominum, in aeternitate temporum,
> in fama rerum.*[61]

NOTES

1. Josephus, *Antiquities of the Jews* 18, 3, 3, §§63-64.
2. Suetonius, *Lives of the Caesars, Claudius* 25, 4.
3. Justin Martyr, *Dialogue with Trypho* 29.
4. Morton S. Enslin, "Once Again, Luke and Paul," in *Zeitschrift für die neutestamentliche Wissenschaft*, Vol. LXI (1970), pp. 253-271.
5. Thucydides, *History of the Peloponnesian War*, I, 22.
6. For a detailed examination of this matter, see my article "Paul and Gamaliel," *Journal of Religion*, Vol. VII, No. 4 (July, 1927), pp. 360-375. Though it was written many years ago, I see no reason to modify the conclusions there expressed.
7. John Knox, *Chapters in a Life of Paul* (Abingdon Press, 1950), p. 34. This is a very rewarding study, to which through the years I have constantly returned and never without profit.
8. Jerome bears witness to a tradition known to him and seemingly the result of chronological confusion, that Paul was born in the Judean town of Giscala, and that subsequent to its capture by Rome his parents moved to Tarsus: *Paulus apostolus, qui ante Saulus, extra numerum duodecim apostolorum de tribu Beniamin, ex oppido Judeae Giscalis fuit, quo a Romanis capto cum parentibus suis Tarsum Ciliciae commigravit* ("Paul the apostle, formerly Saul, not one of the twelve apostles, of the tribe of Benjamin, was from the town of Giscala in Judea, from which town, after it had been captured by the Romans, he migrated with his parents to Tarsus in Cilicia.")—*De viris illustribus* 5.
9. Between A.D. 33-34 and A.D. 62-63 coins from Damascus bearing the imperial image are lacking. The possibility that at this

time Aretas and his successors held sway over the city has not in-frequently been suggested.

10. Phil. 3:5 ("of the stock of Israel, of the tribe of Benjamin"); Rom. 11:1 ("of the seed of Abraham, of the tribe of Benjamin").

11. Augustine, *On the Spirit and the Letter* 12; *Sermons* cclxxix, 5, and cccxv, 5.

12. The fact that when in Rom. 11:1 Paul styles himself, in his mention of his lineage from the tribe of Benjamin, "of the seed of Abraham," may well have suggested to Luke that his hero had suf-fered a change of name at a dramatic moment of his career, as had Abraham before him (Gen. 17:5).

13. Cf. my article "Once Again, Luke and Paul," for this evidence. In this article the question of Luke's probable knowledge and use of the Pauline letters is argued in detail. In this book I have made full use of the conclusions there reached, without always repeating the details.

14. Cf. my *The Ethics of Paul* (Apex Book, Abingdon Press, 1962), pp. 41-43, for a brief description and reference to other discussions.

15. Before the invention of the more convenient Arabic numerals, alphabetic letters were employed: $A = 1$, $B = 2$, $I = 10$; thus $D = 4$ and $ID = 14$.

16. Acts 11:28. For a brief discussion of this date, see F. J. Foakes-Jackson and Kirsopp Lake, *The Beginnings of Christianity*, 5 vols. (The Macmillan Company, 1920-1933), Vol. V., pp. 452-55.

17. Acts 11:27 ff. and 15:1 ff. For a discussion of this problem, see my *Christian Beginnings* (Harper & Brothers, 1938), pp. 226-30.

18. II Cor. 1:12; 2:4; 7:13, 15; 11:23; 12:15; Gal. 1:14; Phil. 1:14; I Thess. 2:17.

19. Cf. George F. Moore, *Judaism in the First Centuries of the Christian Era, the Age of the Tannaim*, 3 vols. (Harvard University Press, 1927-1930), Vol. I, p. 237.

20. But not, if when we read Romans we end it with ch. 8:39, as was my unhappy experience as a student, now fifty years ago.

21. I have made free use in these pages of an earlier article bear-ing this title, "Paul—What Manner of Jew?" which I contributed to *In the Time of Harvest*, essays in honor of Abba Hillel Silver, ed. by D. J. Silver (The Macmillan Company, 1963), pp. 153-69, which I am graciously permitted to use freely.

22. "In Egypt, for example, territory has been set apart for a Jewish settlement, and in Alexandria a great part of the city has been allocated to this nation. And an ethnarch of their own has

been installed, who governs the people and adjudicates suits and supervises contracts and ordinances, just as if he were the head of a sovereign state"—Josephus, *Antt.* 14, 7, 2, §117.

23. "Three years" is far from exact; by the ancient style of inclusive reckoning it may be the equivalent of "two years" or even less.

24. Firmicus Maternus, *De errore profanarum religionum* 22.

25. Adolf Erman, *Die Religion der Aegypter* (Berlin, 1934), pp. 96 f.; Franz Cumont, *Les Religions orientales dans le paganisme romain,* 4th ed. (Paris, Geuthner, 1906), p. 92.

26. Josephus, *Antt.* 20, 2, 4, §§38 ff.

27. It would appear to me probable that Luke's account of Barnabas bringing Paul from Tarsus to Antioch is based on the mention by Paul of Barnabas in connection with the visit.

28. Donald W. Riddle, *Paul, Man of Conflict* (Cokesbury Press, 1940).

29. John Knox, *op. cit.*

30. By their reconstruction, the work in "Syria and Cilicia" is really to be understood to include Galatia, Macedonia, Achaia, and Asia.

31. For a fuller discussion of the nature of the difficulty in Galatia and the opponents against whom Paul is indignantly defending himself, see my *Christian Beginnings,* pp. 218-26.

32. The aorist *espoudasa* is awkward in such a case save as the equivalent of the English pluperfect—"which is precisely what I (we) had gladly done."

33. Apparently "would-be" must be prefixed to this noun in the case of Athens.

34. Cf. *to proteron* (Gal. 4:13). While this word may be understood as "formerly," i.e., prior to the time of writing the letter, it is more likely to indicate "on the former of two occasions," thus suggesting a subsequent visit as well; cf. also chs. 1:9; 4:16, 20; 5:3. A full discussion of the whole problem may be conveniently studied in Ernest De Witt Burton, *A Critical and Exegetical Commentary on the Epistle to the Galatians* (International Critical Commentary) (Charles Scribner's Sons, 1920), pp. 239 ff.

35. "For three sabbath days" (Acts 17:2).

36. II Cor. 1:8 ff.

37. The location of the several churches in Galatia ("I gave order to the churches of Galatia," I Cor. 16:1) is uncertain. Apparently they were in different places in the same general area. When he wrote them, was it a circular letter read in the various communities?

38. George S. Duncan's *St. Paul's Ephesian Ministry* (Charles Scribner's Sons, 1929) is a very useful survey of this problem.

39. For a fuller statement of these oft-debated points, see my *Christian Beginnings,* pp. 263-268.

40. Similarly, for those who regard the imprisonment epistles—Philippians, Colossians, Ephesians, and Philemon—as written from either Caesarea or Rome, there is firsthand evidence from Paul himself that he made the trip indicated. If, however, as has come to be regarded increasingly as probable, these letters are to be seen as coming from Ephesus, that confirmation is definitely removed.

41. Cf. Col. 2:10, 19 with Eph. 4:16.

42. A. D. Nock, *St. Paul* (Harper & Brothers, 1938), p. 134.

43. Ignatius, *Letter,* Ephesians 1:3, 2:1, 6:2; cf. Eusebius, *Ecclesiastical History* iii, 36, 5.

44. The possible identification of Onesimus the slave with Onesimus the bishop of Ephesus has been occasionally mentioned by scholars, but with little enthusiasm. J. B. Lightfoot (*St. Paul's Epistles to the Colossians and to Philemon.* London: Macmillan & Co., 1875, p. 314) dismisses it with a single sentence under the caption, "Legendary history." John Knox has long been an enthusiastic champion of the hypothesis. His repeated treatments of the subject deserve more attention than they seem to have received: *Philemon Among the Letters of Paul* (The University of Chicago Press, 1935); "Philemon" in *The Interpreter's Bible,* Vol. XI (Abingdon Press, 1955), pp. 555-573.

45. E. J. Goodspeed, *The Meaning of Ephesians* (The University of Chicago Press, 1933).

46. Polycarp, *Letter to the Philippians* 3:2.

47. Cf. Rom. 8:38; I Cor. 8:5; 15:24; Col. 1:16; 2:10, 15. The attempt to limit these descriptions to earthly potentates reflects the unwise effort to make Paul share the notions of the twentieth century wherein these supernatural figures find little room or place.

48. Cicero, *De Oratore* ii, 19, 80—*Jubent enim exordiri ita, ut eum, qui audiat, benevolum, nobis faciamus, et docilem, et attentum.*

49. Cf. Rom. 1:20 ff.; I Cor. 6:9 ff.; Gal. 5:19 ff.; Col. 3:5.

50. *c. Neaera* 122, p. 1386.

51. I Thess. 4:3-8. This is the translation by J. E. Frame in his *A Critical and Exegetical Commentary on the Epistles of St. Paul to the Thessalonians* (International Critical Commentary) (Charles Scribner's Sons, 1912), p. 146.

52. Matthew Arnold, *St. Paul and Protestantism* (London: Smith, Elder & Co., 1888), p. 53.

53. George F. Moore, *The Birth and Growth of Religion* (Charles Scribner's Sons, 1923), p. 176.

54. Philo, *De Decalogo* 15 (§73) 193M.

55. Rom. 14:1-23. These ageless words may be read and reread with profit after nineteen hundred years.

56. Col. 3:18 to 4:1, essentially repeated in the later Ephesians (chs. 5:22 to 6:9).

57. The Pastoral Epistles show the next step, while a passage such as Clement of Alexandria, *Paedagogus* iii, 11 f., serves as a handbook of Christian conduct, discussing the proper clothing, the propriety of wearing earrings, finger rings, the use of cosmetics, how to walk decorously, of amusements, even attempting the description of the model maiden—what she should do and what not.

58. Percy Gardner, *The Religious Experience of St. Paul* (G. P. Putnam's Sons, 1911), p. 139. I found this volume of great value when working on my first study of Paul. I find it of equal value today.

59. In this chapter I have drawn heavily upon an earlier study: Morton S. Enslin, *The Ethics of Paul* (Harper & Brothers, 1930; Abingdon Press, 1962), pp. 63-78.

60. For a brief discussion of this too often neglected Pauline champion, see my article "The Pontic Mouse," *Anglican Theological Review*, Vol. XXVII (1945), pp. 1-16; for a more extended treatment, see John Knox's *Marcion and the New Testament* (The University of Chicago Press, 1942), a work of permanent value.

61. Tacitus, *Agricola* 46 (the name of Paul has, of course, been substituted). "Whatever we have loved, whatever we have admired in Paul, abides and is destined to abide in the hearts of men, as the years come and go, in the glory of what he did and what he was."